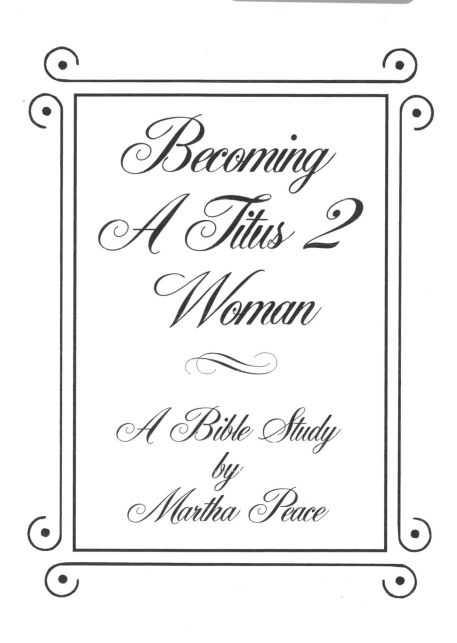

Becoming A Titus 2 Woman

A Bible Study
by
Martha Peace

Becoming A Titus 2 Woman
Martha Peace

Scripture taken from the New American Standard Bible,
© 1960, 1962, 1963, 1971, 1972, 1973, 1975, 1977
by The Lockman Foundation.
Used by permission.

Cover design by Richard Schaefer.

ISBN 1-885904-17-7

PRINTED IN THE UNITED STATES OF AMERICA
BY
FOCUS PUBLISHING INCORPORATED
Bemidji, Minnesota

This book is dedicated to our beloved daughter

Anna Kay Scott

who has brought us so much joy and

who is well on her way to becoming a

Titus 2 Woman.

Acknowledgements

Writing this book was not what I had planned to do this year. Somehow though, Jan Haley from Focus Publishing in Bemidji, Minnesota, talked me into it. Now that it is completed, however, I am grateful for her encouragement and good advice along the way.

The Lord provided me with others to help me as well. My pastor, John Crotts of Friendship Bible Church in Peachtree City, Georgia, graciously and carefully read the manuscript and offered biblically sound advice. He was tactful and kind in the process. His wife, Lynn, edited the manuscript while caring for her husband and their fifteen month old daughter, Charissa. Lynn is especially good with tiny little details, and I am so glad for her help.

Our daughter, Anna Scott, did the initial editing for grammar. I recall that after reading one particular paragraph Anna said, "Mom, this paragraph has no point!" In another incident, she told me that it was not permissible to make my point by saying, "Because I said so." Anna was a joy throughout the process, even though she was very busy caring for her husband and three children. One day I had to iron her clothes in order to give her time to read!

Our son, David, did not really contribute directly to this book, but he asked me, "Mom, am I in your new book?" So, I read to him the section in chapter six where I wrote about David and his fiancée, Jaimee Sumner. I also told him that if I ever (Lord willing) write the Raising Kids Without Raising Cain book, he will be the star!

My husband, Sanford, helped me and patiently encouraged me with my computer problems. When I had finished my writing, he read the manuscript and made corrections. Like David, he also wanted to know if he was in the book. I said, "Of course!"

Barb Smith from Focus Publishing did the final editing. She was not only professional but also offered wise counsel. She has previously served the Lord as a pastor's wife for many years and is now continuing to serve Him through being a Titus 2 Woman to younger women, some of whom are her daughters.

Last, but certainly not least, is Stanley. Stanley Haley is Jan's husband. The two of them are the owners of Focus Publishing. Sanford and I had the opportunity to meet Stanley recently. Stanley told us that in all his years of being in the printing business, he has never had as many equipment failures as he did in trying to get The Excellent Wife book published. We all believe that the Devil would have preferred for Stanley to throw in the towel. However, by God's grace, he did not and now he has agreed to take on another one of my books. Sanford and I are grateful to the Lord for both Stanley and Jan as we serve Him together in these endeavors.

Becoming a Titus 2 Woman

Introduction

Several years ago a church in Augusta, Georgia asked me to do a seminar on developing a Titus 2 ministry. As I thought about the topic and prepared my material, I found myself focusing less on how to organize such a ministry and more on how to become such a woman.

A Titus 2 woman is an older, mature Christian woman who teaches and encourages the younger women. Her ministry is based on the Scripture passage Titus 2:3-5.

It seemed to me that every Christian woman regardless of age or marital status should aspire to become a Titus 2 Woman. It also seemed to me that most churches today are woefully lacking in the training of these ladies. They may have organized women's functions, but there seem to be few if any older women who are discipling the younger women biblically as required in Titus 2:3-5.

Because of the need, I have written this book. Within these pages are many practical examples of how to effectively disciple younger women. It is also practical in its approach to how, by God's grace, we develop the character that He wants every older woman to have.

I must stress that none of what you will read can be accomplished apart from the grace and empowerment of God. We are responsible to pursue righteousness and to obey His Word, but He does the work through the Holy Spirit. He is truly "able to make all grace abound to you" (II Corinthians 9:8). Regardless of your background or what your life was like before Christ, if you are a Christian, God can transform your character and make you into the woman He wants you to be. He alone deserves the credit.

Remember that this process in your growth takes time, work, and prayer. We must often and repeatedly turn to God for His help and enabling power. My prayer is that God will use this book to bless you and use it for His glory. I have written it for Him.

> *And if you address as Father the One who impartially judges according to each man's work, conduct yourselves in fear during the time of your stay upon earth; knowing that you were not redeemed with perishable things like silver or gold from your futile way of life inherited from your forefathers, but with precious blood, as of a lamb, unblemished and spotless, the blood of Christ.*
>
> *I Peter 1:17-19*

Part 1

When I Disciple
A
Younger Woman

Chapter One

A New Philosophy of Life

As a young woman and before I became a Christian, I embraced three philosophies of life. One was the feminist belief that my identity was caught up in my education and career. A second was "eat, drink, and be merry for tomorrow you may die." A third came from the George Burns movie, "Oh, God!" In the movie, George Burns (playing God) said, "Jesus is my son, Mohammed is my son, and Buddha is my son." I thought, "That's it! This makes sense to me. There are many ways to God, and it does not matter what you believe as long as you are sincere."

Believing my identity to be found in education and career, I pursued both with a passion. It did not matter how much I attained through education, I desired more knowledge and more credentials. My nursing career culminated in a teaching position at a local college. My goals were to head the nursing department in a prestigious university and to write a critical care textbook. My standards were high and I would have graduated only the students who were bright and at the top in their field.

The "eat, drink, and be merry" philosophy speaks for itself. I drank and partied hard. I was determined to have fun at any cost. It was supremely important to me to be happy. Needless to say, drinking occasionally got me into trouble and it is a wonder that I was not killed in an automobile wreck. Whereas my feminist "identity" philosophy looked to the future for esteem and accomplishment, this "eat, drink, and be merry" philosophy looked only at the moment with little or no thought for tomorrow.

My third philosophy of life was consistently expressed through membership in a church that was full of people who thought that everyone was a Christian regardless of their beliefs just as long as they were sincere. I was told, "God loves everyone, the Bible is full of myths, and who are we to judge?" That suited me fine, because I certainly did not want anybody judging me.

To my great surprise, these three philosophies did not bring me the satisfaction and happiness I desired. Instead, they brought me heartache, confusion, and desperation to find answers. The answers, however, only came through reading God's Word and praying. One day when I was thirty-one years old, God (in spite of no goodness of my own) drew me to Himself, came into my life, saved my soul, forgave my sins, and gave me a new and different philosophy of life.

My new philosophy is Christian. I now passionately believe that Jesus Christ is the only way to God the Father and that my purpose in life and greatest joy is to serve Him and glorify Him. As I "delight myself in the Lord," God gives me the "desires of my heart" (Ps.37:4). Desires which, by the way, He places there. For example, I remember once praying (because I was afraid I would revert back to my old lifestyle) that God would give me a love for His Word so that no matter how much I learned or knew I would never be satisfied. Even today after over eighteen years, my God-given desire to know and obey God's Word has not diminished.

My new desires include ways to please and serve God. God's instructions on how a Christian woman can please and serve Him are written out clearly in Titus 2:3-5.

> **Older women likewise are to be reverent in their behavior, not malicious gossips, nor enslaved to much wine, teaching what is good, that they may encourage the young women to love their husbands, to love their children, to be sensible, pure, workers at home, kind, being subject to their own husbands, that the word of God may not be dishonored.**

At the time I discovered this passage, I was not exactly an "older woman." But I knew I had so far to go that by the time I learned and applied what I needed, I would be in the "older woman" category. That is what has happened. Though I still have far to go, God is maturing me in three areas: doctrine, character, and ministry for Him.

Because of what God has done and is doing in my life and because of the instructions in Titus 2:3-5, I now have a desire to teach and encourage younger Christian women. That's why I have written this book – to biblically instruct you how, with God's help, you can become a Titus 2 Woman who, in turn, teaches and encourages the younger women. To accomplish my purpose, I have divided the book into four parts:

♦ When I Disciple a Younger Woman

♦ How Does a Titus 2 Woman Act?

♦ What Does a Titus 2 Woman Teach?

♦ Why Should a Titus 2 Woman Teach?

In the next chapter, I explain three areas in my own life in which God first worked so that now I can begin to teach and encourage other women. The three areas were (and still are) doctrine, character, and ministry.

Chapter One
Study Questions

1. Write a paragraph describing what you believe to be the role of the Christian woman.

2. Make a list of the priorities in your life. In other words, what activities and commitments do you have? What takes up your time?

3. Look up the following verses and write down what God's Word teaches us about priorities.

A. Matthew 6:25-33

B. Colossians 3:1-2

C. Romans 12:1

D. I John 2:15-17

E. II Peter 3:18

F. Galatians 6:10

G. Ephesians 5:15-16

4. Pray as you begin this study and ask God to –

■ teach you

■ show you if your priorities are biblical

■ give you a desire to make changes in your thinking or actions that God desires for you to make

■ use this study in your life for His glory

Chapter Two
Three Areas To Mature

Often new Christians have exuberant zeal but very little knowledge. It is common for their desire to serve the Lord to be great but their Christian characters to be woefully lacking. They are like a new student nurse who shows up at the hospital with her crisp, clean new uniform, her shoes polished and buffed, and her hair neatly pinned up off her collar. She is excited and thrilled to be there! She outwardly looks professional and competent. However, looks can be deceiving. Unless she knows her limitations, she can be downright dangerous.

As a new Christian, I was like that young, energetic, enthusiastic nursing student. I wanted to serve the Lord in great ways. I just knew I would soon be like a famous woman Bible teacher of whom I had heard. I learned that her first Bible class doubled in attendance every week. Finally there was no more room for new people.

When I was a fairly new Christian I was approached by a lady in our church named Linda. Linda expressed a desire to host a ladies' Bible study in her home. She said to me, "Will you teach it?" Would I? With boundless enthusiasm I replied, "Yes!!!"

Linda and I invited our friends and neighbors and anyone else who would let us ask them. Our class was held on Wednesday mornings and we began with two or three ladies. I taught the Gospel of John verse-by-verse. Attendance was scanty and erratic. One week in particular stands out in my mind. We had eight ladies definitely commit to attend the following Wednesday! I worked extra hard on my lesson and Linda cleaned and prepared her home. That morning, she got up early and baked homemade sausage biscuits. When I arrived, the smell of the sausage and coffee was wonderful. We were so excited. We prayed and waited expectantly for the guests to arrive.

Soon it was time and eventually past time. Finally, it was so late that we had to face the truth – no one was coming. I felt as if I was going to cry. Linda said, "Maybe the Lord does not want us to have a class." My hope for large groups of ladies coming to hear me teach was being crushed right before my eyes. Rather than cancel the rest of the classes, however, we decided to take a week to pray and then to meet at least one more time.

In the ensuing week, I struggled with what God might be doing. Now, looking back it is fairly obvious what He was doing. He was beginning to mold my character and He was protecting those large groups of women (most of whom by the way, never came) from my immaturity of doctrine and character. I was looking at the moment, God was looking down the road and beginning to prepare me for serving Him. At the time, my zeal without knowledge or character was as dangerous as an unbridled, inexperienced student nurse.

In this chapter, I explain three areas in my own life in which God first worked so that now I can teach and encourage other women. The three areas were (and still are) doctrine, character, and ministry. Let's begin with the first area in which God is maturing me ---

Doctrine

Doctrine is what the Bible teaches about a certain subject. For example, the doctrine of salvation is what the Bible teaches

about how a person can be saved from his sins through the aton-
ing work of Jesus Christ on the cross. Another example is the
doctrine of the Trinity: God is one in three Persons – the Father,
the Son, and the Holy Spirit. When I became a Christian, I knew
very little about what the Bible teaches. So little in fact, I did not
realize that what I was *thinking* could be a sin. Through Bible
study and reading God's Word, I learned much more about the
doctrine of sin than I even knew was possible. Obviously, if God
were going to use me to eventually teach other women, I had a
great deal to learn.

As a new Christian, I began to read and study the Bible. I
also read good books and listened to Bible study tapes. I had
pastors who helped me by answering my questions, by sug-
gesting good study books and commentaries to read and use,
and by letting me teach a ladies' Bible study class at church or
in someone's home. I had to learn how to "handle accurately
the word of truth" (II Timothy 2:15).

It took me fifteen months to teach that first Bible study class
on the Gospel of John! Each week, I prepared the lesson and
wrote homework for the ladies as well. The next year, at the
suggestion of my pastor, I taught Genesis. In subsequent years,
I taught the prophets, Esther, Colossians, Romans, Malachi, and
Revelation.

Since those original classes, there have been times when I
have retaught certain subjects and as I restudy previous material, I realize that my understanding of certain doctrines is maturing. It is an on-going process for all Christians. At my pastor's
request, he reads each of my lessons before I teach it to our ladies. He then corrects any misunderstandings that I have or any
Scripture that is taken out of context. Teaching under his authority is a true blessing and protection for me as well as subsequently for the other ladies in our church. The more I learn, the
more I realize how much I do not know. Even though I have

been teaching the Bible now for nearly fifteen years, my understanding of doctrine continues to mature.

Knowing doctrine is a critical foundation to a ministry of teaching and encouraging the younger women but would be of little use if God had not begun to mature my character.

Character

Whether you want to describe the maturing of my character as "pruning me so that I can bear fruit" (John 15:2) or as disciplining me so that I can "share His holiness"(Hebrews 12:10), changing my character has been the most difficult and most personally humiliating of the three areas. The bad news is that it is sometimes embarrassing to realize you are less than perfect. The good news is "God gives grace to the humble" (James 5:6).

One of the areas in my character that needed drastic changing was the character quality of anger. Anger surfaced when I did not have my way or when something or someone irritated or frustrated me. I was one of those "angry men" (or women in my case) you should not go with "lest you learn his ways and find a snare for yourself" (Proverbs 22:25). Instead of being easily irritated, impatient or openly angry, God began to change me into a woman with a gentle and quiet spirit.

I remember once speaking intensely to another woman in our church. She and her husband were thinking of leaving and going to a church which I knew to be doctrinally unsound. Instead of responding to her in a gentle and loving tone, I became too intense and harsh. They subsequently left our church; but I justified what happened in my mind because, after all, I was right. Not long after the incident, a mutual friend of ours called me on the phone. She was very nice but straightforward. She said, "I agree with what you said, but your tone with her sounded harsh and angry. The Bible tells us that if we are to rightly influence others whose doctrine is wrong, 'the Lord's bondservant must not be quarrelsome, but be kind to all, able to teach, patient when wronged, with <u>gentleness</u> correcting those who are in opposition...' (II Timothy 2:24-25). One reason they have left is because of your harshness."

Needless to say, I was embarrassed and very upset to hear her reproof. I cried and when I hung up the phone, I prayed. I asked God to help me understand. I pleaded with the Lord to make me a gentle woman. I thanked Him for the telephone call. I then decided to go to the other woman and ask her forgiveness.

Because it was Christmas time, I stopped and purchased a poinsettia plant for her. As I approached her front door, I was hoping that she would not be home so that I could just leave the plant with a note of apology asking for her forgiveness. However, she <u>was</u> home and invited me in. I tried to break the ice by telling her that I had brought her a "Peace Poinsettia." (No pun intended!) I asked her to please forgive me because of my harshness and she very graciously did so. They did not, however, come back to church.

I have learned that instead of angry bullying to try to achieve God's ends, only loving gentleness pleases Him. It was not enough for me to recognize and "put off" my harshness and impatience, I had to "put on" love. For example, I should have conveyed my thoughts but I should have expressed them in a godly, gentle tone.

God has changed my character and much more often than not, I am by His grace a gentle person. When I am not, I return to the basics (I John 1:9). I think through how I should have responded, ask God's forgiveness, and the other person's forgiveness. I pray that next time, I will think <u>first</u> and then respond in love.

Another area in my character that required work was becoming less selfish and more loving. "Love does not seek its own way" (I Cor. 13:5) was very convicting to me. God gradually showed me through Scripture and the conviction of the Holy Spirit that I was to seek His way and not my own. As He has matured me, pleasing Him has brought me very great joy.

In addition to becoming more gentle and less selfish, there was a great need within my character to be humble. Instead of being defensive, God wanted me to carefully listen and at least consider what the other person was saying. Instead of focusing on having been hurt from the reproof, He wants me to grow and learn from it. There is no more vivid example in my life than what happened when I wrote <u>The Excellent Wife</u> book.

Because I knew I would be a fool to write a book, especially a book about the doctrine of being a godly wife, without help and scrutiny, I asked for help. The Lord gave it to me! Four separate men, three pastors and one biblical counselor, read it and made comments. The result was a tremendous amount of work and time writing and rewriting. Making some of those changes was like being asked to give up my baby. Every word I had written was precious to me. However, not every word I had written made good sense or was biblically accurate. Because of my sinful pride, I became overwhelmed and at one point seriously threatened to throw the entire project in the trash! Obviously this was not a mature response. The next day as I thought about my impulsive reaction, I was ashamed especially because of all the help the Lord had provided. I realized that it was much more important to the Lord that I "walk humbly with Him" than that I ever write a book (Micah 6:8).

God is still working on all these character areas and many others that I have not included here. He had to mature me to a certain point so that I could begin to teach and encourage the younger women. It is truly a testimony of His goodness and mercy and grace for what He has done in my life.

Certainly, as I had to become more mature in my doctrine <u>and</u> my character, I also had to mature in my ministry or service for the Lord.

Ministry

My service for the Lord has gone through several phases. Now it is focused on my home with my husband and in our church with a ladies' Bible study class as well as discipleship/ counseling of ladies within our church. As time permits, I speak at ladies' seminars and write.

I remember learning a very hard lesson about what God did and did not want me to do. Several years ago, I had a passionate, deep desire to become a missionary. In fact, I just <u>knew</u> it was God's will for us to sell everything, forsake almost all our worldly possessions, and go (of course) to Africa! I was just thrilled even thinking about it. That had to be the ultimate in serving the Lord.

After much prayer and still feeling very fervent, I talked with my husband, Sanford. I was so excited and enthusiastic as I explained that he could quit his job, we could sell our house, and go wherever the Lord wanted. I asked him to please "think about it." He nicely said, "I don't need to think about it. I am *not* quitting my job. We are *not* going anywhere. I believe the Lord wants us here to serve in our church."

Well, I was crushed. How could I ever be as holy as someone who gives up everything to go to Africa? As I thought about it and prayed, I came to understand that God's will for me, at least for the time being, was to be graciously and joyfully under the authority of my husband.

In addition to my disappointment over not getting to be a missionary, there are many times while serving the Lord when I must do something that I think I am not particularly gifted to do. Some examples are playing the piano at church, organizing meals to be carried to someone who has had a death in the family, or staying in the nursery. Regardless, I am to serve the Lord joyfully and "bear fruit in every good work" (Colossians 1:10).

I know what and how much time to commit through the guidance of Sanford and the other elders in my church. They willingly share me with other churches on a limited basis, but they believe (rightly so) that my primary service should be to my husband, then to the ladies in our church, and finally to others.

Regardless of what our spiritual gifts may be, I believe that God desires every Christian woman's ministry to be somewhat centered around <u>being</u> a Titus 2 Woman (married or single) and <u>teaching and encouraging</u> the younger women to be a Titus 2 Woman. In the next chapter, I will explain some general biblical principles in discipling other women as well as give you some specific examples of women with whom I have worked.

<u>Editor's Note</u>: As we go to press, Martha Peace and her husband, Sanford, are visiting South Africa, where Martha is teaching ladies how to develop the character of God and become "Excellent Wives."

Chapter Two

Study Questions

1. According to chapter two, list three areas in which God matures Christian women.

2. Define the term "doctrine." Give two examples.

    Do you consider yourself to be doctrinally mature? If not, what could you do to remedy the situation?

3. Take a few minutes to think about the areas in your character in which God desires to mature you. List them here.

4. Make a list of the ways in which you are serving the Lord.

5. The Lord Jesus said in John 15:8, "By this is My Father glorified, <u>that you bear much fruit</u> . . ."(emphasis added). In order for you to bear fruit, what must happen first? Read John 15:1-6.

6. Pray and ask God to prune you so that you may bear fruit for Him.

Chapter Three

Examples of Discipling Younger Women

When I was a girl of about twelve my mother offered to teach me and my best friend, Anna Owen, how to sew. She took us to a fabric shop and let us choose patterns and material. I remember that my material was a beautiful pink and white striped polished cotton. It had a glossy, candy-like appearance. Since it was summertime, I chose a pattern for a sun-dress.

Mother patiently showed us how to lay out the patterns, cut out the dresses, and then sew them together. Although I did not think about it at the time, there was a great deal of love and joy for my Mother in what she was doing. I learned a lot about sewing even though I do not recall ever having the courage to wear that dress in public. Perhaps I did once. Mother, in a sense, was being a Titus 2 Woman to us. She was an older woman teaching the younger women how to care for their families and be sensible with money. As a result, she gave me a legacy that is part of me today. Although I do not have much time to sew, I still enjoy it when I can.

Just as my Mother had a desire to teach me and my friend Anna, God has given me a desire to teach the younger women how to do many things. Instead of sewing, however, I desire to teach others to "love their husbands, love their children, be kind, sensible, pure, workers at home, and be subject to their own husbands" (Titus 2:3-5). In order to accomplish this goal, when

I have a Titus 2 relationship with a younger woman, I become personally involved in her life. She is my friend. I share personal things with her and we help each other become as much like the Lord Jesus Christ as possible.

Sometimes we meet together on a scheduled basis such as once a week. Other times, we simply talk on the telephone or meet for lunch. We may meet together to discuss a good Christian book we are both reading. Maybe she desires an older woman to pray with or perhaps to teach her how to pray. It could even be that she needs someone to teach her how to sew, shop for groceries, or clean her house. Depending on her areas of weakness and strength, I disciple and hold her accountable in the three areas in which God has in the past and still is maturing me: doctrine, character, and ministry.

Discipling In Doctrine

My experience has been that most of the Christian women I disciple have very sound doctrinal beliefs. When told the definition of a particular Bible doctrine, they readily agree. However when asked to explain the same doctrine in their own words without first being told the answer, they are often unable to clearly explain it and cannot think of a Scripture to prove their point. So, with the assistance of our pastor I have written short, simple definitions with two or three Scripture references for each core doctrine. I usually ask the ladies I am discipling to write their own definitions using their own words. This also includes verbally saying the definitions, looking up the Scriptures, and pretending to explain them to someone else. I ask them to speak aloud and perhaps even practice with someone else to make sure they are being clear. Once I had a public speaking teacher in college who required us to practice aloud. Her point was that even if we were nervous, we would be much more likely to give a clear presentation. I did not know it then, but it is actually biblical to "teach your mouth how to speak" (Proverbs 16:23). Women need to be doctrinally sound and teach other women in a clear, biblical manner.

Discipling In Character

Often I will ask a younger woman, "What sins or what character weaknesses do you think God wants you to work on?" They might reply something like, "pride, anger, fear, gossip, or selfishness." Once I asked a woman what she thought her sins were. She could not think of any, so I asked her this, "If I could ask your husband what he would like for you to change, what would he say?" Quickly, she gave me quite a list!

Another time I asked a woman what sin in her life needed work and she was very vague about what sin even was. So, I read to her the deeds of the flesh (which the Bible says are obvious): "...immorality, impurity, sensuality, idolatry, sorcery, enmities, strife, jealousy, outbursts of anger, disputes, dissensions, factions, envying, drunkenness, carousing, and things like these..." (Galatians 5:19-21). We did not proceed past the first one, immorality, before she stopped me and asked me to help her.

Frequently, the older woman will have observed an area in which she believes the younger woman should work. If so, the older woman should lovingly but in a straightforward manner tell the younger woman of her observations. Once it is determined what sins from which the younger woman must turn, find or write a Bible lesson for her to study or books to read that you can discuss one chapter at a time. At this point, encourage her to put off her sin and put on a righteous response in its place. Ask her weekly how she is doing and talk about how she should have responded when her thinking or verbal response was sinful. This is a good time to begin learning about the specific list of godly character qualities she is to develop in Titus 2:3-4. (These qualities will be covered in detail in chapters three and four.)

Discipling In Ministry

Every Christian woman should be serving the Lord Jesus Christ in some way. Paul wrote to Timothy that the woman's adornment should come "by means of good works, as befits women making a claim to godliness" (I Timothy 2:10). Very often, a large portion of her ministry is to her husband and family through caring for them and praying for them. Ask these questions, "What do you think your spiritual gifts are?" or "If you could do anything for the Lord, what would you want to do?" She may have a definite idea of something she would like to do. Perhaps it is to teach a Sunday School class but she does not know how. She may have a desire to organize meals for the sick or be hospitable to visitors or out of town guests to the church. Maybe she has a heart to visit those in nursing homes or use her talent to sing in the choir. Regardless, it is likely that her desires have come to her from God through spiritual gifts or natural talents that He has given her. In fact, it may be feasible for her to begin serving the Lord right away at a lesser level than her full desire.

It is also possible that God has given her desires that will be fulfilled in a way she has not imagined. For instance, I have never become a missionary but have had many opportunities to teach, help equip, and pray for women who are. I may never actually go to the mission field, but God is none-the-less using me indirectly on the mission field to serve Him on behalf of others. Just as it was probably not God's will for me to go to Africa, or I was not ready, the younger woman may not be ready to teach a Sunday School class for five-year-olds because she does not have patience with the children or sound Bible knowledge. While she is putting on the character qualities of patience and is learning the doctrine, she can still observe one of the experienced teachers or serve as an aid in her class.

Once, I helped a younger woman who had a desire to teach our ladies' Bible study. With the permission of the elders, I gave her small teaching assignments (perhaps a five or ten minute segment in my lesson that she would prepare and I would review with her). I taught her how to organize her own lessons and teach them in a clear and coherent manner. She practiced and I lovingly critiqued her content and delivery. Eventually, she taught an entire lesson and then a series of lessons. Even though she was already gifted by God, she and others benefited from the little bit of help I gave her.

Serving the Lord is God's will for every Christian –

> *"For we are His workmanship, created in*
> *Christ Jesus for good works, which God*
> *prepared beforehand, that we should walk in*
> *them."*
> *Ephesians 2:10, emphasis added*

It is the older woman's biblical responsibility to walk in good works such as teaching and encouraging the younger women by discipling them in all three of these areas – doctrine, character, and ministry.

Examples of Discipling Younger Women

Mrs. Hensley

Mrs. Hensley is like the Pied Piper. She meets one evening every other week with young women from her church and community. She is teaching them Bible-based material on raising kids. She never stops. When she gets to the last lesson, she starts over. Young women cycle in at any time and her class has grown by leaps and bounds. She is a precious lady and the younger women love her. She takes care and time on each lesson. In fact, they stay on one lesson as many weeks as necessary until they understand it. More importantly, the younger women are growing in their love for God as they see the Scriptures explained practically and they implement them in their lives.

Emily

Recently, Emily had an opportunity to disciple her daughter-in-law in raising children. Emily lovingly prepared her lesson and went over it with Melinda each time they met. She encouraged Melinda and gave her the gospel. Once I met with Melinda and asked her if she was a Christian. She said, "I am not a Christian yet but Emily is helping me to become one." In the meantime, they are both seeing the fruit of godly, consistent discipline in three-year-old Zachery's life.

Maribeth

Maribeth is a forty-nine year old single lady. She has never been married and works as a computer analyst for a large corporation. At work, she is surrounded by younger women, some of whom gravitate to her with their problems or just for Christian fellowship. Whether it is romance questions like whether to continue dating a particular young man or a problem with a non-Christian husband, Maribeth has learned to go to the Scriptures to answer their questions and to give them hope. She has had the joy of seeing the Lord work in several young women's lives. Maribeth would prefer to be in a "professional" ministry, but God is using her for His glory right where she is!

Sandy

Sandy teaches a Sunday School class of about twenty ladies. She teaches them and shares her life with them. They frequently call her to help with their problems. Sandy is currently taking a course on biblical counseling to better prepare herself to answer their questions practically and give them guidance. It is obvious how much Sandy loves the Lord and she is a joy to be around. Now that her children are almost grown, she has much more time to reach out to other women and she is using that time wisely.

Conclusion

No matter what you are teaching the younger woman -- how to sew, know clear sound Bible doctrine, be godly in character, or to serve the Lord through some sort of ministry to her family, church, or friends, God wants the older women to teach and encourage the younger women. I have found it helpful to have some sort of organized method. Regardless of the younger woman's strengths or weaknesses, I try to help her in all three of the areas mentioned in this chapter – doctrine, character, and ministry. Obviously, some require more help in certain areas than others. My goal is to help them mature to the point that with God's help they begin to serve others in a way that is pleasing and honoring to the Lord Jesus Christ.

In the first three chapters, I have explained the broad overview of the areas in which I disciple younger women. These are all areas in which God has and is continuing to mature me. The areas of doctrine, character, and ministry are what we cover

<u>when</u> I disciple other women. Now, I want to proceed to the second part of this book – <u>How</u> does a Titus 2 Woman Act?

Chapter Three

Study Questions

1. One of my goals is for you to become thoroughly familiar with Titus 2:3-5. To help you , take the time to write out Titus 2:3-5 in the following space.

2. Read over what you wrote in question number one and <u>think</u> about it carefully. What is Paul saying? How could you explain it to someone else? Write Titus 2:3-5 again except this time phrase it in your own words.

3. According to Titus 2:3-5, what should the older woman be like? In other words, how did the Apostle Paul describe her character?

4. From Titus 2:3-5 make a list of <u>what</u> the older woman is to teach and encourage the younger woman to do.

5. If an older woman were discipling you, what would you want her to do?

6. In Titus 2:3-5 Paul was very specific about the role of the older woman in the life of the younger woman. In a general sense, all Christians are to minister to one another. Look up the following verses and write out some of the other ways women are to be involved in each other's lives.

A. Galatians 6:2

B. Matthew 22:39

C. I John 4:7

D. I Peter 4:9

E. Hebrews 3:13

F. I Thessalonians 5:14-15

G. Galatians 6:10

Part 2

How Does A Titus 2 Woman Act?

Chapter Four

Her Character

~~~

When an older woman befriends a younger woman, she is likely to influence the younger woman's thinking and actions. That can be good news or bad news. For example, it is bad news when the older woman leads the younger woman into heresy. It is good news when the older woman is doctrinally sound. It is bad news when the older woman rebels against the authority of the elders in her church or her husband. It is good news when she is graciously under their authority. It is bad news when the older woman is a gossip. It is good news when she is like the "holy women of old" (I Peter 3:5).

Obviously, God does not want an older woman to be a bad influence on the younger Christian women. Instead, He wants her to have the godly character listed in Titus 2:3-5.

> *"Older women likewise are to be <u>reverent in their behavior, not malicious gossips, nor enslaved to much wine, teaching what is good,</u> that they <u>may encourage the young women</u> to love their husbands, to love their children, to be sensible, pure, workers at home, kind, being subject to their own husbands, that the word of God may not be dishonored" (emphasis added).*

This chapter explains how a Christian woman can have the character of the Titus 2 woman. Regardless of her age now, she can eventually become an older woman who truly does "teach what is good" and "encourage the young women" (Titus 2:3-4).

The Characteristics of the Older Woman Reverent in Her Behavior

The Greek word for reverent is *hieroprepeis*. It is two Greek words put together to make one word. *Heirps* means sacred or sacred services. *Prepei* means proper, to be fitting. Behavior is the word *katastema* meaning demeanor or behavior or deportment. (Deportment is how you act.) [1] In other words, you behave in a proper manner. The King James Version of the Bible expresses it beautifully, "behavior as becometh holiness."

Matthew Henry described this type of a woman as one whose "behavior becomes a woman consecrated to God." [2] She should act and dress in a manner pleasing to God. She should be outwardly different from the world and holy within.

Reverent in Her Dress and Attitude
and
Reverent in How She Acts

How can a godly woman be "reverent in her behavior?" One way is by how she dresses. She should dress in a feminine manner, not like a man. She should be modest, not sensual and provocative. She should enjoy the freedom she has in the Lord to wear make up and dress pretty but not be ostentatious and vain. Rather she should adorn herself by her good works as Paul wrote to Timothy:

> *"Likewise, I want women to adorn themselves with proper clothing, modestly and discreetly, not with braided hair and gold or pearls or costly garments; but rather by means of good works, as befits women making a claim to godliness."*
> *I Timothy 2:9-10*

One time I spoke to a ladies' group at a church where the women believed that it was a sin for a Christian woman to wear jewelry. On the surface of Paul's letter to Timothy, it may seem that they are correct. However, the Apostle Paul is not saying in I Timothy that women are not to braid their hair or wear jewelry. Paul was writing to Timothy whom he had left in Ephesus as a pastor to the new church. In Ephesus, the temple prostitutes were known for their gaudy, suggestive, vainglorying, extreme styles for their hair and jewelry. Unbeknownst to the prostitutes, their only beauty was surface and empty. Paul did not want the Christian women to look like the worldly women. They should be different. So, what this passage means is that a Christian's manner of dress should be free from ostentation. If she is going to stand out, it should be because of her good works done quietly.

Peter wrote of a similar concern to Christians scattered throughout the world. In I Peter 3:3-4, he addresses the proper adornment of a godly woman.

> *And let not your adornment be merely external – braiding the hair, and wearing gold jewelry, or putting on dresses; but let it be the hidden person of the heart, with the imperishable quality of a gentle and quiet spirit, which is precious in the sight of God.*

In this passage, Peter (like Paul) could not be saying a woman cannot wear braided hair and gold jewelry. If he were, she would be forbidden to wear dresses, too! Rather what he is saying is that her external adornment should not be her emphasis. Her true beauty comes from what is on the inside – a "gentle and quiet spirit." This kind of gentleness is a meekness. It is accepting God's dealings with her as good. She does not resist nor dispute with God. In addition to a gentle heart, she has a quiet spirit; one that is peaceable and tranquil. She is not given to anger or fear.

Her attitude is like the "Excellent Wife" in Proverbs 31. Her attitude towards the future shows her reverence and quiet trust in God. She is "not afraid of the snow for her household, for all her household are clothed with scarlet." She is clothed with strength and dignity as she "smiles at the future" (Proverbs 31:21,25).

We have a godly, precious young couple in our church. One day, Duane and Cynthia's basement was flooding with water because their sump pump had stopped working. She became very distraught and phoned her husband at work and asked him to come home and repair it. He told her that he could not leave but that he would instruct her how to repair the ailing pump. She did not handle it very well even though he very patiently explained to her what to do. She finally relented and did as Duane asked. Lo and behold, the pump began to work! Later, her husband called back to see if she had (by God's grace) regained her "gentle and quiet spirit" (I Peter 3:5).

This is an extraordinary example of a loving husband who was trying to help his wife be reverent in her behavior. Instead of being offended by his inquiry, a truly godly wife would be grateful for the gentle reminder. In addition to husbands reminding their wives to have the proper, reverent attitude, the older women should be reminding the younger women also. In fact, they themselves should be "reverent in their behavior" (Titus 2:3).

Let me summarize the point. Godly women reflect reverence in their behavior by dressing in a manner that is not sensual, provocative, masculine, or excessively gaudy and ostentatious. Instead, their adornment is their good works and their gentle hearts and quiet spirits. The attitude of their hearts (what they think) is pleasing to God. In addition, a godly woman is…

Reverent in How She Acts

Another way a godly woman is reverent in her behavior is by how she acts. She shows love to others by remembering that "love is not rude" (I Corinthians 13:5). She has good manners. She does not push and shove in the department store. She does not embarrass herself and others by yelling at the store clerk and making loud threats when circumstances are not going her way. She is not loud and obnoxious and rolling over people like a steam roller. Plainly put, she behaves herself. She is a proper lady at home and in public.

I want to clarify something here. Being "reverent in her behavior" does not mean she whispers when she talks, hides in the background, or does not look at others when they talk. I used to know a woman who did whisper when she talked and I remember thinking, "she is so sweet and feminine and godly." That is what I thought before I really got to know her character! It turned out that she is mean as a snake, but she certainly whispers sweetly as the venom is coming out of her mouth.

In contrast, women who are actually reverent in their behavior enjoy life. They laugh and speak loudly enough for others to hear. They do not have a false idea of spirituality. They have fun and love the Lord. They want to make others comfortable. They show love to others by acting properly as they rejoice in every day that the Lord has made. Their dress, attitude, and behavior are pleasing to the Lord. They are a modernized version of the "holy women of old" (I Peter 3:5).

So, the Titus 2 woman is to be reverent in her behavior. She is also not to be a malicious gossip.

Not A Malicious Gossip

"Not a malicious gossip" is *me diabolous* in Greek. *Diabolos* is the same word translated Devil or Satan. It means to "accuse, to repudiate, to give false information, to be a talebearer." [3] Obviously, gossip is a grievous sin. Often, it is the socially acceptable sin. It is so easy to let that one little tid-bit of information out especially if you are upset with the other person. An older woman must have integrity regarding the information that the younger woman gives her. Her focus should be to help the younger woman respond righteously to those who have hurt and offended her. The Titus 2 Woman guards her words carefully, does not talk too much, and gives godly counsel but does not gossip.

Guards Her Words Carefully

"Women must likewise be dignified, <u>not malicious gossips</u>, but temperate, faithful in all things" (I Timothy 3:11, emphasis added).

Yesterday I went to the Post Office and ran into a lady from my Bible study class. Her son had broken his leg very badly and we were discussing what had happened. An older gentleman came in and got in line behind us. I realized that he thought we were in line and we were not so I said, "Sir, we are not in line, we are just talking." He laughed and said, "I know how women are. I have five sisters and I was the only son. I also have a wife and four daughters!" He was teasing us, but he had a point. Women do enjoy talking. Of course there is nothing wrong with talking <u>unless</u> they do not guard their words carefully.

The biblical criteria for the words you say could be summed up with three principles: speak edifying words, speak truthful words, and speak good report words.

Edifying Words

Let no unwholesome word proceed from your mouth, but only such a word as is good for edification according to the need of the moment, that it may give grace to those who hear."
Ephesians 4:29

Edifying words build up the other person. They are not a false, manipulative form of giving praise. They are spoken for the purpose of helping the other person be strong in the Lord or to help them become more like the Lord Jesus Christ. They may be encouraging or they may be a reproof. It depends on what would be appropriate. Such words are honoring to the Lord and have an eternal purpose and worth.

The Titus 2 Woman must be steeped in the Scriptures if she is going to truly edify others. Her desire would be to help the other person be like Christ. She would be sensitive to the "need of the moment" (Ephesians 4:29). The purpose of her words is to "give grace to those who hear" (Ephesians 4:29). Her words are good and beneficial to the hearer, not unwholesome. The underlying meaning of unwholesome is rotten. Consider the following examples of "rotten words (unwholesome)" compared to "beneficial words (good)."

The Titus 2 Woman speaks edifying words. Her words give grace to the other person. They are not unwholesome. They are also truthful.

ROTTEN WORDS	GOOD, BENEFICIAL WORDS
"Sue, your husband is stupid! That is the worst thing I ever heard."	"Sue, the Lord wants you to give your husband a blessing instead of returning evil for evil." I Peter 3:11
"If I were you, I would leave him. I certainly would not let him treat me like that."	"I know your circumstances are hard, but if you must suffer, suffer for doing what is right."
"Guess what I heard about Judy?"	"Guess what I learned from the Bible today?"
"Let me tell you the details of the sex scene in this book I read."	"Let me tell you what I read in R.C. Sproul's book, The Holiness of God."
"#*!!@#. That makes me furious!"	"Thank you Lord for this test. Help me to respond in love."

Truthful Words

Therefore, laying aside falsehood, speak truth, each one of you, with his neighbor, for we are members of one another.

Ephesians 4:25

Paul wrote to the church in Ephesus that it was not enough to stop lying. They were to tell the truth. Sometimes we do not tell an outright lie but in essence we lie by leaving out part of the story or by being deceitful in some other way.

I have had clients when I worked at the Atlanta Biblical Counseling Center who blatantly lied to me. Sometimes the results were tragic because I gave counsel based on what I thought to be true. My counsel would have been different had I known the truth.

Other clients did not openly lie, but took more of a "If she doesn't ask, I won't tell" tactic. Obviously, they were being just as deceitful as those who spoke the lie. Like some of my clients, it is so easy to be a malicious gossip by leaving out part of the truth or, of course, by telling an outright lie. Instead, the words we speak should be truthful.

One word of caution however: realize that even when you are telling the truth, you can still be gossiping and painting the other person in a bad light. You would be giving a bad report instead of a good report.

Good Repute Words

As you guard your words carefully, consider whether what you are about to say is of "good repute" (Philippians 4:8). Good repute thoughts (and subsequent words) do not lead to slander and gossip. They think of the other person's reputation in a favorable light. These thoughts are the kind of thoughts we are to carefully consider and think about. Otherwise, it is so easy to let a bad report out and become what Titus 2:3 warns against – a malicious gossip.

If there is something about the person that would paint them in a bad light, go to the person and speak to them about it. Your demeanor should be gentle and loving, but truthful, clear, and straightforward. Give them hope. Do not give a bad report. Do not gossip. In addition to guarding your words carefully, …

Don't Talk Too Much!!!

When there are many words, transgression is unavoidable. But he who restrains his lips is wise.

Proverbs 10:19

I know that I am not the only one who is guilty of talking too much. If you continue to talk long enough, you are likely to say something you should not have said. It is so easy to overstep the bounds of what is right. Instead, a godly woman has self-restraint. She goes <u>to</u> the person, she does not talk <u>about</u> the person. How can a younger woman or anyone for that matter trust you if you are not wise with what you say?

There is a Christian woman who has a reputation for being a gossip. She not only tells things but she tries hard to find out information. She is not above calling others and asking direct questions about someone else that are clearly none of her business. You must be on guard against people like that. If you are not careful, before you know what happened, you will have said more than you should have. Stand up to gossips, say something like, "If we continue to talk about this or I continue to listen to you talk, we are likely to begin to gossip." So, ladies, talk, but do not talk too much!!

You may be thinking, "I do not want to gossip, but what should I do if another woman wants to talk to me about a problem she is having in a relationship and she does not know what to do." Suppose she comes to you and has a problem with her friend at church. First determine if her desire is to respond righteously. If so, listen to just enough to give her biblical guidance such as, "You need to go to your friend and gently confront her with her sin. Your motive should be to restore her to a right relationship with God" (Galatians 6:1). Show her appropriate Scriptures and point out her responsibility.

If she comes back to you and wants to talk about it again but does not want to talk to her friend, then do not listen but explain, "Last time we talked I listened to enough information to give you biblical guidance. Now if we continue to talk about it, we'll just be gossiping." Then encourage her to do what is right, pray with her, and follow up later by asking her if she did. But do not let yourself be pulled into gossip.

Gossip is a besetting sin of far too many women, old and young. We must all be on guard to speak edifying, truthful, and good report words. Plainly put, it helps not to talk too much. When it is appropriate to give godly counsel, focus on the responsibility the younger woman has to biblically respond to others. Begin now to cultivate the character of a Titus 2 Woman who is not a malicious gossip.

As we have seen, the Titus 2 woman is not to be a gossip and she is to be reverent in her behavior. That is not all. She is a woman who is "not enslaved to much wine" (Titus 2:3).

Not Enslaved to Much Wine

It seems that on the island of Crete in the Apostle Paul's day, there was a larger than normal problem with women drinking too much. Even sweet little old grandmothers can be drunkards!

Contrary to many popular notions today, drunkenness is a sin. It is one of the deeds of the flesh listed in Galatians 5. It is listed as characteristic of an unrighteous person who "will not inherit the kingdom of God" (I Corinthians 6:9). To be "enslaved" is the Greek word *douleuo* which means "to be a slave, to serve, or to be in bondage." [4] *Douleuo* comes from the word *doulos* which means to be a slave. The Bible teaches us that we come into bondage to that which we serve – either our own sinful flesh or the Lord Jesus Christ.

Paul admonishes all Christians to "behave properly as in the day, not in carousing and <u>drunkenness</u>, not in sexual promiscuity and sensuality, not in strife and jealousy. But (instead) put on the Lord Jesus Christ, and make no provision for the flesh in regard to its lusts" (Roman 13:13-14, emphasis and adaptation added). Obviously, a woman enslaved to wine would be "next to useless" trying to help someone else. She would be pathetic. Thankfully, a Christian woman enslaved to wine can by God's grace repent and turn from her sin.

Ladies, alcohol is not to be a problem in your life. If you drink enough ethyl alcohol (the addictive ingredient in alcoholic beverages) you will desire and crave more and more. It will eventually snare you and you will be caught in a trap that no matter how much more you drink, it will never be enough. If it is a problem for you, confess your sin to God, remove any temptation from your home, seek godly biblical counsel, and seek accountability. If you humble yourself and get help, God will give you the grace to pursue righteousness. The day will come when alcohol is no longer a temptation or an issue. I know because I was once in bondage to alcohol. Now I do not even think about it. God has so changed my character that it is not a problem.

We all choose whom to obey. Some obey the Lord and others obey their fleshly cravings and desires. Consider what Paul wrote to the Roman church members:

> *Do you not know that when you present yourselves to someone as slaves for obedience, you are slaves of the one whom you obey, either of sin resulting in death, or of obedience resulting in righteousness? But thanks be to God that though you were slaves of sin, you became obedient from the heart to that form of teaching*

to which you were committed, and having been
freed from sin, you became slaves of
righteousness.
Romans 6:16-18

All day long every day you make choices about what you will think about or do. Think of it as a matter of obedience. If you obey God, you will not "carry out the desire of the flesh" (Galatians 5:16). It will mean, at times, you will not always be able to do what would please you (Galatians 5:17). If alcohol is a problem, the pull of your flesh will be great but as you obey God and ask Him for strength and guidance and direct your thoughts to more lofty desires such as prayer for others, God will gradually make it easier and easier for you to resist your sinful self. Eventually, by His power, you will have victory over drunkenness.

Many of you are probably not plagued with drunkenness. However, there is a secondary application. You can be enslaved to other things such as television, food, romance novels, or prescription drugs. Just because something may be "lawful" such as prescription drugs does not mean it is profitable. Paul explained by saying...

All things are lawful for me, but not all things
are profitable. All things are lawful for me, but I
will not be mastered by anything.
I Corinthians 6:12

Being mastered by anything other than the Lord Jesus Christ is a serious sin, but by God's grace, you can repent. Paul wrote to the church at Corinth and warned them sternly that drunkards (and others) would "not inherit the kingdom of God" (I Corinthians 6:10). Then came the astounding news, "And such <u>were</u> some of you; but you were washed, but you were sanctified (made holy), but you were justified (declared righteous by

God) in the name of the Lord Jesus Christ, and in the Spirit of our God" (I Corinthians 6:11, adaptation added).

Instead of pursuing wine or food, use that same energy to think about God – His goodness, mercy, and holiness. Think about and plan ahead how He might want you to glorify Him with the same energy it would have taken you to pursue that to which you are in bondage. Ask yourself, "For Jesus' sake, what do I want to do with this block of time?" The answer is usually obvious – "Whether, then, you eat or drink or whatever you do, do all to the glory of God" (I Corinthians 10:31, emphasis added).

Conclusion

In this chapter, we have considered three characteristics of the Titus 2 woman. She is reverent in her behavior, not a malicious gossip, and not enslaved to much wine (or anything else for that matter!). She is mature and stable and not out of control. She is a woman whom the elders in her church could depend upon to be a good influence over the younger women. She is a woman who continues to work on these qualities in her life and continues to ask for God's wisdom, conviction, and grace. God has laid within her the foundation of godly character that she needs in order to teach and encourage the younger women.

Chapter Four

Study Questions

1. What does it mean to be "reverent in her behavior?"

2. How are women to be adorned?

   A. According to I Timothy 2:9-10 –

   B. According to I Peter 3:3-4 –

3. What does it mean to have a "gentle and quiet spirit?"

4. Write down two or three examples of unwholesome words
    that you have said. (See Ephesians 4:29.) Now write down
    what you <u>should</u> have said – words that are good and
    beneficial.

5. In Philippians 4:8, we are told to think thoughts that are of
    "good repute." What does that mean? Give two examples.

6. Explain what you should do if another woman approaches you for advice about her friend who is sinning.

7. What might a woman be in bondage to besides alcohol?

8. Reread Romans 6:16-18. Is there anything that comes to mind to which you are in bondage?

9. What is your prayer?

Chapter Five

Her Response to the Younger Woman

Older women likewise are to be reverent in their behavior, not malicious gossips, nor enslaved to much wine, <u>teaching what is good</u>, <u>that they may encourage the young women</u> to love their husbands, to love their children, to be sensible, pure, workers at home, kind, being subject to their own husbands, that the word of God may not be dishonored.

Titus 2:3-5, emphasis added

Older women are instructed in Titus 2 to teach and encourage the younger women. Often, the older women will discern actions or patterns of thinking in the younger women that are sinful or foolish. They will pray for the younger women but do nothing else. Why? A common answer seems to be "If I say anything, she will get mad at me." This reminds me of the line in the song that goes "Oh, dear, what can the matter be?"

The "matter" is likely due to wrong thinking and responses on the part of the older woman <u>and</u> the younger woman. The older woman may be afraid that something unpleasant might transpire. She probably grew up with the belief that you do not say anything unless the other person asks for help. On the other hand, the younger woman may be proud and become defensive if anyone thinks she is less than perfect. She probably grew up with the belief that if anyone reproves her they are not accepting her as she is, not loving her, and making her feel badly.

Obviously, this is a problem because God intends the older woman to teach and encourage the younger woman. The process should be as natural as slipping your hand into a glove that fits perfectly. If both will do what is right – the older one reaching out in love to the younger and the younger one responding in humility with a teachable heart – God will be glorified, the older woman will overcome her fear, and the younger woman will grow in grace by leaps and bounds.

Instead of complaining about or being afraid of the younger women, the older Christian women should pray for them, involve themselves in their lives, and whether privately or in a classroom setting, teach and encourage the younger women. The rest of this chapter and book explains how.

Teaches What Is Good

"Teaches what is good" is a combination of two Greek words resulting in one word. *Didaska* means "an instructor, theoretical and practical knowledge." [5] We get our English word, didactic, from the Greek word. The second word, *kalos*, means "good, commendable, excellent, honorable, right, or sound." [6]

I remember a time when I was a young woman, and as a new Christian I was struggling in a particular area of submission to my husband. I knew I was sinning and I confessed the sin on a regular basis. However, it kept recurring. Finally, I decided to seek help. As I thought about whom to ask, I thought of Dori.

Dori was an older woman in my church who knew God's Word well and seemed to me to be a sterling example of a biblically submissive wife. I telephoned her and asked if I could come to see her. We planned to meet in her home the following Tuesday. It was winter and she had piping hot spiced tea brewing. As we drank our tea, I explained my struggle.

She asked me, "Why did you come to me?" The answer was simple, "Because I knew you would tell me the truth." And she did, lovingly but in a straightforward manner from the Scriptures. The Lord used her in my life to teach me "what was good." She was a wonderful example of the older woman in Titus 2 who was described by Matthew Henry as a woman who "by example and good life...gives doctrinal instruction at home and in a private way."

How can you become a woman like Dori who teaches what is good? You must begin by –

Studying Sound Doctrine

All Christians are instructed to work hard studying the Scriptures. Paul wrote to Timothy to be ...

> *"...diligent to present yourself approved to God as a workman who does not need to be ashamed, handling accurately the word of truth."*
> *II Timothy 2:15*

As we said earlier, doctrine is what the Bible teaches about a certain subject. It is so important that women study diligently so that they will not be ashamed and will also not be "carried about by every wind of doctrine" (Ephesians 4:14).

Instead of being "carried about," women should study the passages on women, wives, and mothers, but they should also study the character of God, the doctrine of salvation, and the doctrine of sin. They should in a practical sense know how a Christian is to "put off anger...and instead be kind, tenderhearted, and forgiving" (Ephesians 4:31-32). They should know in detail how to pursue love as "Love is patient, love is kind," etc. (I Corinthians 13:4-7).

Diligently studying God's Word is a command of God. The Bible is unlike any other book. It is inspired by God in a unique way. It is "alive and powerful" (Hebrews 4:12). It can be used to protect us from the Devil himself. Consider how the Lord Jesus responded to Satan as Satan tempted Him in the wilderness:

> *It is written, "Man shall not live on bread alone, but on every word that proceeds out of the mouth of God."*
>
> *Matthew 4:4*

Also consider Job. Job was a man who longed for God as he "treasured the words of His (God's) mouth more than my necessary food" (Job 23:12, adaptation added).

Learning and applying Bible doctrine makes us wise ("Thy commandments make me wiser than my enemies..." Psalm 119:98). It is the mark of a true disciple ("Jesus therefore was saying to those Jews who had believed Him, 'If you abide in My word, then you are truly disciples of mine...'" John 8:31). It guarantees our complete equipping ("All Scripture is inspired by God and profitable for doctrine...that the man of God may be adequate, equipped for every good work" II Timothy 3:16-17).

You must study the Bible and learn to use it rightly in context if you are going to truly teach "what is good." Attend weekly Bible studies that are doctrinally sound and full of meat. Do not waste your energy on shallow share time. Read good, doctrinally sound books. Read the Bible and meditate on what it means.

Thoroughly learn the passages on women and other important doctrines. Until you have them memorized, write a note
somewhere in your Bible with references to which you may easily refer as you talk with others. The following is a copy of a
page of references I looked up, typed up, and taped to one of
the front pages in my first study Bible.

DOCTRINE	REFERENCES
Inspiration of Scripture	II Timothy 3:16-17 II Peter 1:20-21 John 5:46-47 John 17:17
The Gospel	Romans 3:23; 6:23 Isaiah 53 Ephesians 2:8,9 John 3:16,17 I Peter 2:24 II Corinthians 5:21 Acts 26:19-20
Assurance of Salvation	I John 5:10-13 John 6:47 John 3:16, 18, 36 Romans 10:9, 10, 13 Titus 1:2
Jesus is God	John 14:7 John 10:25-30 Titus 2:13; 3:4 John 1:1,14
Wives and Submission	Titus 2:3-5 Ephesians 5:22-24,33 I Peter 3:1-7 Colossians 3:18

A Titus 2 woman studies the Word of God diligently. She is like my friend Dori who opened her Bible, instructed me, and explained how I could practically apply doctrine in my life. Dori not only had studied the doctrine and "handled it accurately," she was a model before me of living out the doctrine in her life.

Modeling Before Them

In addition to teaching what is good, a Titus 2 Woman is also to live out Bible doctrine in her life. She respects the governing authorities (I Peter 2:17), she shows respect to the pastors of her church (I Thessalonians 5:12-13), and she respects her husband (Ephesians 5:33). She has the attitude of being _for_ her husband or the younger woman's husband, not against them (Proverbs 31:12). She is like the "Excellent Wife" in Proverbs 31:12 who "does him (her husband) good and not evil all the days of her life" (adaptation added).

She admits when she is wrong because she is a humble woman. She readily asks forgiveness. She does not overreact if others think she is less than perfect. It is not the end of the world and her feelings are not hurt and her life ruined if she has been reproved. She truly understands that the "wounds of a friend _are_ faithful" (Proverbs 27:6, emphasis added). She is more concerned with glorifying God than in looking good or being proven right. She knows her heart is deceitful and she wants to be pruned and molded by God. As a result, God pours out His grace to her and uses her mightily for His glory.

In addition to being humble before God and others, a Titus 2 woman uses her spiritual gifts. Whether possessing the gift of teaching, exhorting, organizing, or mercy, she rightly uses her gifts not for self-edification but for their intended purpose of building up the body of Christ (Ephesians 4:12). She also unselfishly uses the talents God has given her and is generous like the "Excellent Wife" in Proverbs 31 who "extends her hand to the poor; and she stretches out her hands to the needy" (Proverbs 31:20).

A godly older Titus 2 woman does much more than just <u>live</u> a godly life, she <u>talks</u> about the Lord; and she especially talks <u>to</u> the younger women about Him. She does not have to possess the official gift of teaching to teach the younger women. She does not hold to the view "my faith is private. I just let my life show my faith." Certainly, her life <u>does</u> model her faith but she also speaks up and out in love as she "teaches what is good" (Titus 2:3).

In addition to teaching the younger woman, she...

Encourages the Younger Woman

Encourage is the Greek word *sophronizo*. It means "to recall one to his senses, to admonish (warn), to exhort, to spur on." [7] *Sophronizo* comes from the root word *sophron* which means "of sound mind, prudent, self-controlled, sensible." [8]

Sophronizo encompasses more than just the greeting card mentality of "I'm thinking of you today" or "Just a note to say 'Hi.'" It is encouraging the younger woman to make the sensible choice. It may include energetically urging or warning her to do what is right.

This kind of encouraging is the bedfellow of teaching what is good. In other words, it takes both teaching <u>and</u> *sophronizo*. It reminds me of the Apostle Paul. He was gifted by God as a master teacher of doctrine but intertwined throughout his teaching was "beseeching, warning, reproving, praying, urging, exhorting, and encouraging." (See Colossians 1:28-29 and Acts 20:18-21,31)

Like Paul, the Titus 2 woman encourages (in the *sophronizo* sense) the younger woman by learning how to give reproofs.

Loving Biblical Reproofs

Brethren, even if a man is caught in any trespass, you who are spiritual, restore ("to lift him up, to mend") such a one in a spirit of gentleness, each one looking to yourself, lest you too be tempted.

Galatians 6:1, emphasis and adaptation added

And if your brother sins, go and reprove him in private; if he listens to you, you have won your brother.

Matthew 18:15, emphasis added

Being reproved or admonished is embarrassing for anyone. The younger woman is no exception. Make it as easy for her as you can by speaking to her privately (if possible). Do not approach her in a self-righteous manner such as "How could you do that?" or "I would never do that." Instead, be gentle and speak in a kind tone of voice.

Your motive should be to restore her to a right relationship with God and others. It is for God's glory, not for proving you are right. You are not "nailing" her but loving her, desiring what is best for her.

Pray for wisdom from God and prepare what you are going to say since "the heart of the wise teaches his mouth and adds persuasiveness to his lips" (Proverbs 16:23). Think about what you want to say before you start talking. If you believe the subject may be difficult for the younger woman, write out what you want to say and practice it aloud.

Depending on the circumstances, you may need to gather more information <u>before</u> you reprove or admonish her. You might discover that a reproof is not in order after all. It is shameful and foolish to "give an answer before you hear..." (Proverbs 18:13).

If an admonishment or reproof is necessary, cradle it with hope. Use Scriptures such as I Corinthians 10:13, Romans 8:28-29, and Proverbs 27:5-6. You must believe that there truly is nothing that has happened that God cannot forgive and that He will begin to mold her character (and habitual responses) to His standard expressed in His Word. It might be appropriate to say something to her like, "There is nothing that has happened that God cannot forgive you for and others should not forgive you for. Would you think about what I've said and pray and ask God to make it clear to you?"

Be wise if you are working with a new Christian. God's standard is the same for all Christians but choose your "battles" wisely and be patient. For example, a new Christian may be struggling with bitterness towards her husband, not being disciplined in keeping house, and inconsistency in disciplining her children. Out of these three, my initial focus would be on helping her with her bitterness towards her husband (Ephesians 4:31-32 and Romans 12:17-21). Next would be her inconsistency with disciplining her children (Ephesians 6:1-4). The last priority would be keeping an organized house (Proverbs 31:22, 27; Titus 2:5). Be wise and give them time to assimilate what they are learning.

For example, suppose you talk with a young Christian woman whose church attendance has been erratic. She explains some of the problems she is having with her children and with getting organized. You give her a few tips such as:

◆ On the Thursday before Sunday, wash your family's clothes and iron the pieces you will need for Sunday.

◆ Stay home on Saturday evening. Before you put the children in bed, lay out their clothes (including hair bows, socks and shoes) for the next morning.

◆ Set your alarm early enough to give you extra time to work with the children if someone spills their milk.

At church the following Sunday you wait with anticipation for her arrival and she does not show! What should you think? Assume the best -- that she was providentially hindered. Perhaps she has a sick child. Should you even inquire? Sure, but approach her in love and find out the facts first.

Consider another example of an older woman biblically encouraging a younger woman. In this example she follows the biblical pattern in II Timothy 3:16-17.

All Scripture is inspired by God and profitable for <u>teaching</u>, for <u>reproof</u>, for <u>correction</u>, and for <u>training in righteousness</u> ; that the man of God may be adequate, equipped for every good work (emphasis added).

Example of Encouraging a Young Woman

1. Use Scripture to **teach** her biblical principles on receiving reproof. Proverbs 15:31-32 (For more information on receiving reproof see <u>The Excellent Wife</u> book.[9])

2. **Reprove** her in a kind but clear manner. Give specific examples. For example, "Sue, I know it is very difficult when your children are young, but I believe I have noticed a pattern of sin in your life when you are correcting your children. Sometimes you speak to them in a harsh, angry tone of voice."

3. Explain how she can **correct** this fault. "It might help if you discipline them the first time you give them an instruction and they do not obey. If you keep telling them, you are much more likely to become angry and they are much more likely not to take your instruction seriously. Also, it may help to practice what you are going to say to them aloud. Before you speak, think something like 'Love is patient. I can show love to her by instructing her, speaking in a gentle tone of voice.'"

4. **Training in righteousness** is a process that must occur over and over until it becomes part of the younger woman's character. It takes time and practice. Meanwhile, the older woman should continue to biblically, lovingly, and patiently encourage the young mother.

Giving a loving, biblical reproof is not fun nor is it necessarily pleasant. As I mentioned earlier, it is likely to be embarrassing for the younger woman and not the greatest joy for the older woman. If the older woman is more concerned about what others think of her or with feeling comfortable than she is with helping the younger woman, she will probably talk herself out of doing what she now knows is right. Consider the following examples of selfish thoughts compared to godly, loving thoughts.

SELFISH THOUGHTS	GODLY, LOVING THOUGHTS
"She will get mad at me."	"I do not know that she will be angry but if she does get angry, God will give me the grace to go through it and to help her."
"She will leave the church."	"It will be unfortunate if she leaves the church, but it will be the consequences of her own sin."
"It will not do any good."	"Only God can know if it will do any good. Whether she glorifies God in her response or not, I can glorify God by obeying His Word to biblically reprove her and thus help the younger woman."
"It would upset me if she got angry or pulled away from me or talked about me to others."	"She may respond better than I think possible. Most people do when we approach them God's way. Regardless, my responsibility is to do what the Lord requires of me. If I have to feel uncomfortable in the process, I will just have to feel uncomfortable. I am going to show love to her instead of being selfish."

Sophronizo is not only warnings and reproof in a negative sense. It is also positive. Give the younger woman appropriate praise and encouragement. Tell her (when appropriate) "I am glad you put the Lord first. It is an encouragement to me to see what God is doing in your heart and life." "I know what you are experiencing right now is difficult but every day that you endure you are showing love to God." "You did a good job. Thank you very much."

Sophronizo is also praying for the younger woman and sometimes baby-sitting. It is checking on her to see if she needs anything when her husband is out of town. It is a small "I was thinking of you while shopping" gift for her. It is remembering her birthday. It is being a model before her of a woman like the "holy women of old" (I Peter 3:5).

Conclusion

Sophronizo is much more than "greeting card," vague, fuzzy encouragement. It is praise and encouragement that includes warnings when appropriate. It is "recalling one to his senses." It <u>will</u> be done by an older woman who loves her Lord. It will <u>not</u> be done by an older woman who is selfish and loves herself more than she does others. It <u>will</u> be done by an older woman who is mature in doctrine and knows how to "teach what is good." It will <u>not</u> be done by an older woman who is doctrinally ignorant or is "carried about by every wind of doctrine."

Chapter Five
Study Questions

1. Since the older women are to teach sound doctrine to the younger women, take the following test of your knowledge of Bible doctrine.

   Instructions: Give two or three Scriptures (without looking in your Bible or concordance) for each of the following subjects:

   A. The Bible is inspired by God.

   B. Jesus is God.

   C. We cannot earn our salvation. It is given to us by God through His grace.

   D. Wives are to be submissive to their husbands.

2. Unless you scored exceptionally well on the last question, make up a chart similar to the "Doctrine/References" chart in this last chapter. You may compose your own chart or use/borrow from mine. If you use mine, look up and think about each Scripture. In addition to writing your answer in this book, place your chart some where in your Bible for a ready reference.

3. What should the Titus 2 woman's attitude and response be
    if confronted by someone who thinks she is wrong?

4. Explain what the Greek word *sophronizo* means.

5. What might prevent you from giving a needed biblical
    reproof?

6. According to Galatians 6:1, what should your motive be when reproving someone else?

7. Reread the examples of selfish thoughts from Chapter five that you might be tempted to think when faced with the occasion of giving a biblical reproof. Then reread the godly, loving thoughts. Which way would you normally tend to think?

8. What is your prayer?

Part 3

What Does A Titus 2 Woman Teach?

Chapter Six

To Love Their
Husbands and Children

Titus was a Gentile convert to Christianity who had traveled with the Apostle Paul. After a few years, Paul left Titus on the island of Crete (off the coast of Greece) in order that he might minister to the churches there. Later, Paul wrote the letter we now call Titus to instruct Titus on what to teach to the people in the churches on Crete.

In this letter Paul especially wanted Titus to know the role of God's grace in promoting good works among God's people. There were instructions for –

◆ the older men

◆ the older women

◆ the younger men

◆ the younger women

◆ the slaves

The older women were to be "reverent in their behavior, not malicious gossips, nor enslaved to much wine..." (Titus 2:3). In addition, they were to "teach what is good and encourage the young women" to –

1. love their husbands

2. love their children

3. be sensible

4. be pure

5. be workers at home

6. be kind

7. be subject to their own husbands

These seven very specific instructions were <u>what</u> the older women were to teach. This chapter explains the first two of the seven instructions –

1. to love their husbands

2. to love their children

But first I want to explain who these "older women" are.

The Greek word for "older women" is *presbutidas*. This word means literally "aged women, the elder women." [10] They may have been plentiful on the island of Crete but in our churches today they do not seem to exist. As I have visited various churches, I commonly hear the younger women tell me, "we need help but there are no older women here who will help us."

It is somewhat of a puzzle why this is such a problem. It may be that the older women were never taught this material when they were young. Some may be vain and not want to be considered in the older woman category. Others may wrongly believe that once their children are grown and out of the home they have done their part and have no further responsibility. Often their lives reflect a feminist viewpoint of seeking fulfillment and "identity" from more education or career.

Others selfishly put all their time and energy into their own children and grandchildren. They do not reach out to anyone else. Many believe that it is not their place to be involved with other women in such a personal way. As was mentioned earlier, the older woman may be afraid the younger woman will be offended or react angrily. I do not know all the reasons but I do know that in most of the churches I visit, the younger women are begging for godly, older, mature women to help them.

Most of the rest of this book is about <u>what</u> the godly, older Titus 2 woman is to teach. We will begin with teaching them to love their husbands. Included in this section are practical examples of how the Titus 2 Woman can teach the younger woman to love her husband with *philos*, *agapao*, and "one flesh" love.

Teaching Them to Love Their Husbands

"To love their husbands" is *philandros*. This one Greek word is a compound of two words – *philos* and *aner*. *Philos* is one of the words for love in the New Testament. It means "beloved or a dear friend." [11] This kind of love indicates a tenderness. *Aner* means "man, gentleman, or husband." [12] So, it is to be fond of one's husband or consider him to be a dear friend. In the South, we might tell a wife to cultivate a "sweetness" toward her husband.

Teaching Them Philos Love

The best way to teach the younger women to love their husbands in a *philos* way is to begin with what the Bible teaches about wives loving husbands. Wives are not commanded directly in Scripture to love their husbands. However, they are instructed indirectly through the older women teaching them and encouraging them to do so.

The older women can help the younger women show *philos* love to their husbands by encouraging them to think and act in the following ways.

EXAMPLES OF THINKING *PHILOS* THOUGHTS
1. "He is so dear to me."
2. "Look at him reading to the children. How sweet."
3. "I must remember to tell him what happened today."
4. "Perhaps I can find someone to watch the kids this evening and we could take a walk and talk after he comes home from work."
5. "I love him so much."
6. "I know we do not have much money right now but he works so hard to provide for us. He is showing love by trying so hard."
7. "What a joy that we can share this time with the children together. He is a good father."
8. "I know he is tired and has had a hard day at work. I think I will give him a back rub."
9. "I know this week is going to be especially difficult for him. What can I do to make it easier for him?"

10. "I know his brother got angry and ruined our dinner party, but my husband cannot help that. I feel badly for him that his brother made a fool of himself."

11. "I know he does not always show love to me as he should but he does not know the Lord. Therefore, he has no capacity to love others as he should."

EXAMPLES OF DOING *PHILOS* ACTIONS
1. Hold his hand while walking through the shopping mall.
2. Offer to invite your husband's family over for dinner even though you would rather be doing something else.
3. Cut the grass for him during a week when you know he will be especially tired.
4. Write an unexpected card of appreciation to your husband for all that he has done for you.
5. Arrange a surprise weekend for the two of you to go off together to rest and talk.
6. Carefully prepare meals that are nutritionally sound and pleasing to your husband's appetite.
7. Express to him how much he means to you and how glad you are he is in your life.
8. Work as hard or harder at being a good friend to your husband as you work at being a friend to your girl friends.
9. Look for practical ways to treat him as someone special and beloved.

Teaching Them Agapao Love

In addition to loving their husbands in a tender, beloved, "dear to her" sense, wives are also to love their husbands in an *agapo* sense. In other words, all Christians are to love others sacrificially. The Lord Jesus Christ is our supreme example.

> *Therefore be imitators of God, as beloved children; and walk in love, just as Christ also loved you, and gave Himself up for us, an offering and a sacrifice to God as a fragrant aroma.*
> *Ephesians 5:1-2, emphasis added*

When we deny ourselves what we would actually prefer and thereby show love to another, we are being a living sacrifice. We sacrifice ourselves for what God would want. It is like a pleasing sacrifice (an aroma) to God.

Teaching Them "One-Flesh" Love

In addition to *philos* love and *agapao* love, a husband and wife are given a special one flesh bond by God. Being united in "one flesh" includes their physical union but not exclusively. It is primarily an emotional bond that grows from the revealing of themselves one to the other. This reminds me of a young couple I know who often go for walks down their country road or sit out in their yard in the gazebo and talk. Their love is growing and maturing as they tell each other how they feel and what they think. They may not always agree and their thoughts may be at times unbiblical, but they are helping each other grow in the Lord as they grow in their one-flesh bond to each other.

About a week ago at this writing, our son David became engaged to a lovely Christian girl. Watching them together is great fun! They look at each other with a special tenderness. They laugh and whisper. They are definitely cherishing each other. For the time being I do not have to remind Jaimee to think of David as someone special and beloved. However, when they (Lord willing) have been married for ten years, I may need to remind her. My desire is that by God's grace I would love Jaimee enough to help her to *philandros*, to love her husband.

As we have seen, the older women are to teach and encourage the younger women to love their husbands. Now, let us consider how the older women can teach and encourage the younger women to love their children. Included in this section are practical tips for the Titus 2 Woman to employ – teach her to think loving thoughts, hold her accountable to be kind and tenderhearted, teach her to express affection and delight in her children, and teach her how to lovingly administer godly discipline.

Love Their Children

The Greek word for "love their children" is *philoteknos*. This word is a combination of the word *philos* (beloved, tenderness) and *teknos* (child). The idea is for the mother to think of her child as beloved or dear. Paul conveyed a similar idea in I Thessalonians 2:7-8 as he defended and illustrated his care over the new converts in Thessalonica.

> *But we proved to be <u>gentle among you, as a</u>*
> *<u>nursing mother tenderly cares for her own</u>*
> *<u>children.</u> Having thus a <u>fond affection for you</u>,*
> *we were pleased to impart to you not only the*
> *gospel of God but also our own lives, because*
> *you had become very dear to us.*
> *I Thessalonians 2:7-8, emphasis added*

Most mothers love their children. In fact, most would die for their children. It seems to be inherent in mothering for the mother to tenderly care for her child. My pastor's wife, Lynn Crotts, had her first baby last year. No one had to tell Lynn to hold Charissa carefully when she picked her up. No one had to say, "Be sure and kiss her and hug her and keep her clean and feed her." I never lost a minutes sleep for fear Lynn would not lovingly care for her precious baby because Lynn loves Charissa. The Lord had placed in Lynn's heart a tender cherishing for her child even before Charissa was born. I remember Lynn telling me before Charissa was born, "I cannot wait to see her little face and to hold her." Lynn was already thinking of her child in a tender, beloved way.

Before our daughter Anna's first child was born, she asked me to come to Greenville, South Carolina to help her when the time came. She also said, "I really will need your help with the house, cooking, and laundry, but I want to be the one to take care of the baby." She was already anticipating mothering her child, and she was anxious to learn how. Tommy was brought home to a fully stocked nursery that Anna and Tom had lovingly decorated. Anna tenderly talked to Tommy, sang to him, fed him, bathed him, changed him, and prayed for him. She proudly showed him off. She quickly developed her mothering skills. As much as she loved Tommy before he was born, she loved him more as the days went by.

When Anna and Tom's twin girls, Jordan and Kelsey, were born, I saw that same tender, cherishing love. It bothered her when she had to go home from the hospital two weeks before the girls could go home. Again, the nursery was ready. The challenges this time, however, were enormous compared with Tommy's birth! Tommy was barely two. This time Anna appreciated the help of anyone who would assist with the care of the babies. She was in survival mode but in spite of the challenges, Anna maintained her tender, cherishing mother's love for her children.

I wish I could tell you that every mother, including Lynn and Anna, always feel and show a tender love to their children but you would know that is not true. All mothers struggle to one degree or another with impatience. Some are even mean and hard-hearted. Some selfishly neglect their children. Regardless of how little or how much they love their children, all mothers could benefit from occasional help and encouragement. As an older woman teaching and encouraging the younger mothers I would...

Teach Her to Think Loving Thoughts

Encourage the younger mother to memorize I Corinthians 13:4-7. "Love is patient, love is kind, etc." She should learn it so well, she could easily rattle it off her tongue. Next, she should take each individual action of love and write out loving thoughts and/or actions towards her children. You want her to develop a habit of thinking biblically loving thoughts such as "This is awful being up most of the night with my sick child but I can speak to her in a gentle, kind tone of voice since 'love is kind'" (I Corinthians 13:4). Consider another example – "I wish he would hurry up trying to tie his shoes but the truth is I do have time to wait, and as I wait patiently I am showing love to him because 'love is patient'" (I Corinthians 13:4). "My feeling is that if I have to stop what I am doing one more time and spank her, I'll scream. However, I know I can by God's grace do what is right and show love to her since 'love is not provoked ... and love endures all things'" (I Corinthians 13:5,7).

Showing love is so very important that the first and foremost commandment is to love God with all your heart, soul, mind and strength (Matthew 22:38). The second most important commandment is to love others (Matthew 22:39). It is no wonder that the Apostle Paul prayed for the Christians in Ephesus that they would be "rooted and grounded in love" (Ephesians 3:17). It is also no surprise that the Apostle Peter wrote that even in the midst of suffering we are to "keep fervent in our love for one another" (I Peter 4:8).

Since we are commanded in Scripture to "pursue love" (I Corinthians 14:1) and to put on a heart of compassion and love (Colossians 3:12-14), a mother should work very hard at this. Replacing selfish and unloving thoughts comes by God's grace and diligent work on the part of the mother. As she disciplines herself in this area, God will change her character and she will love her children from her heart in the way God desires. In addition, the older woman should hold the young mother...

Accountable to be Kind and Tender-Hearted

When I was a young mother I was also a nurse. I worked in a pediatric intensive care unit at a large charity hospital. We only had four beds but they were usually full of very critically ill children. In a typical day, life or death hung in the balance. I was trained to perform life-saving (but often painful) procedures on the children. They cried and fought but I had to proceed anyway knowing that I was ultimately doing the most kind act I could for them. As a result, I developed a certain kind of callousness towards my own children. When Anna or David would come running with their little hurts and skinned knees, I would clean the wound and say something like, "Stop crying. You're all right." In my mind, anyone who could breathe <u>was</u> all right!

When I became a Christian, I continued to work as a nurse for a while. One day while overseeing student nurses in the Coronary Care Unit, I observed the wife of a man who had had a very serious heart attack. He was not doing well and she came in to visit him. I did not know either one of them and had never seen them before. As the wife was walking out of the unit, she began to weep. My heart went out to her and I, too, began to cry. My reaction surprised me as it was so different from how I would have reacted before I became a Christian. God clearly had given me a new heart with new desires. I was learning to be tender-hearted and compassionate.

Many mothers are like I was – more hard-hearted than tender-hearted. They do not naturally <u>feel</u> sympathetic when their child has some minor trauma or injury. However, as Christians they can learn to express compassion and will eventually begin to feel it. Instead of saying, "Oh, you are all right!" she can say, "I am so sorry that you hurt your knee. Let me see it. I know that must really hurt."

In addition, to saying, "I am so sorry..." or "I feel bad that you hurt yourself," a young mother could study Scriptures on compassion. Often it is expressed in the King James Version of the Bible as "tender mercies." She should meditate on appropriate verses, learn from the example of the Lord Jesus Christ, and pray and beg God to make her a more compassionate, tender-hearted mother.

Often there is a connection between not being tender-hearted and being malicious. Malice is being mean. I believe that a large portion of what the world calls "verbal abuse" is what the Bible calls "malice." A mother with malice in her heart makes cruel fun of her child, calls him names, twists the truth, overreacts with physical discipline, speaks in a harsh tone of voice, and often tries to control her children with anger. She is mean and believes she is justified in her meanness. When exasperated, the mother lets "unwholesome words" out of her mouth instead of edifying words (Ephesians 4:29). Her responsibility before God is to put off the malice and put on kind, tender-hearted, and forgiving thoughts and actions.

> *Let all bitterness and wrath and anger and clamor and slander be put away from you, along with all malice. And be kind to one another, tender-hearted, forgiving each other, just as God in Christ also has forgiven you.*
> *Ephesians 4:31-32*

MALICIOUS THOUGHTS AND ACTIONS	KIND, TENDER-HEARTED, AND FORGIVING THOUGHTS AND ACTIONS
1. "That makes me so mad!"	1. "Lord help me to be patient with Jordan since she is too young to have good muscle coordination."
2. "You are selfish!" (said in a very harsh, angry tone of voice)	2. "This child is not a Christian. I cannot expect her not to think of herself first. I need to teach her from Scripture about love."

3. "I am tired. Leave me alone!"	3. "I am tired and wanted to sleep late, but Nathan is hungry and so happy to be up this morning. I <u>can</u> get up and prepare his breakfast."
4. "I wish he had never been born!"	4. "Lord, thank you for this child and for helping me with the responsibility."
5. "Hurry up. You are so slow!"	5. "It is not right when I get up late and take it out on Caleb. It is not his fault."
6. "I should have known better than to expect you to make your bed correctly."	6. "Tommy, let me show you once more how to smooth your bed covers properly. Then I am going to mess them up and let you try. It is all right if you cannot do it as well as I do, but you must try really hard."
7. "You are stupid!"	7. "Kelsey, I know this is hard to understand but I want you to listen carefully and try. I am confident you can succeed."
8. "I hate you."	8. "I love you."

It is not uncommon to see a mother grab her child in anger in the grocery store or in the church. Even mothers who are normally easy going and tender-hearted can be exasperated beyond belief! Of course, they never have an excuse to sin before God and to sin against their child but they do need help. The older women are to lovingly hold them accountable to be kind and tender-hearted instead of mean and hard-hearted. Another way the older women can help the younger women to love their children is to remind them to be wise like God.

> *But the wisdom from above is first pure, then* _peaceable, gentle, reasonable, full of mercy and_ _good fruits,_ *unwavering, without hypocrisy. And the seed whose fruit is righteousness is sown in peace by those who make peace.*
> *James 3:17-18, emphasis added*

This particular passage in James is especially convicting to me. The word "reasonable" is translated "easy to be entreated" in the King James Version. The word for peace is *eirene* which means "harmony of relationships."[13] It should not be traumatic or frightening for a child to come to their parent with a respectful request. The mother's heart should be full of mercy and very gentle even if she does not grant the child's request. Every child who grows up in a Christian home should be able to look back on that experience and think of their mother as one who was "full of mercy" and "easy to be entreated."

House rules are often a point of conflict between children and mothers. They are certainly necessary but it is critical how they are enforced. Sometimes young mothers become like Marine drill sergeants at boot camp. As a result, the rules are enforced in a cruel and hard-hearted way through threats, screaming, yelling, and name calling. It may result in an outwardly compliant child who remembers to make their bed and take off their muddy shoes, but it is also likely to produce a child who is likewise cruel and hard in their heart. Gentleness and mercy are more important than external rules. Help the young mothers to be consistent with enforcing house rules but to do it in love. If they must err, it should be on the side of mercy since "...mercy triumphs over judgment" (James 2:13).

In addition to teaching, encouraging, and holding the young mothers accountable to be kind and tender-hearted, the older women should encourage them to ...

Express Affection and Delight in their Children

The attitude of Christian mothers should be the attitude of the Lord.

> *Behold, <u>children are a gift of the Lord</u>; the fruit of the womb is a reward. Like arrows in the hand of a warrior, so are the children of one's youth. How blessed is the man whose quiver is full of them; they shall not be ashamed, when they speak with their enemies at the gate.*
> *Psalm 127:3-5, emphasis added*

The older women should teach the younger women God's perspective on children. They are a precious gift from Him to them. Often I say to the little children at church, "God gave you to us as a gift and I am so glad!" And of course I tell them, "I love you so much!!!"

Hugs and kisses should be routine. Lynn's baby, Charissa, is only twelve months old. She already knows how to blow you a kiss. As she does, you can see the joy in her eyes. The reason is that she has been kissed so much by her family, our church family, and me!

The everyday, ordinary Christian life should be one of joy in what the Lord is doing. Mothers, too, should be looking forward to what God is going to do in their lives and the lives of their children. The older women should be an example for and an encourager to the younger women to live their lives in a way that would draw and not repel the children from an interest in the Lord. They should have the same attitude the Lord Jesus Christ had:

> *Then some children were brought to Him so that He might lay His hands on them and pray; and the disciples rebuked them. But Jesus said, "<u>Let the children alone, and do nothing to hinder them from coming to Me;</u> for the kingdom of heaven belongs to such as these."*
> *Matthew 19:13-15, emphasis added*

There is no place in the Christian faith for anything other than tender, cherishing love and joy for children. From what I can understand from my mother, her grandmother was very expressive, smiled and laughed easily, and paid special attention to children.

"Nonnie" would sing to the children, dance around the room with them, and tell them, "You are so beautiful!" Nonnie was a Christian. She read her Bible and talked about the Lord and taught the Scriptures to her children. She took them to church. My mother fondly remembers "Nonnie took time with me. She would play games with me and pay attention to me." She was still memorizing Scripture in her eighties.

Nonnie died when I was six months old so all I have is a picture of her holding me. Actually, I have more than that. I have a legacy that was passed down to me of *expressive joy* in children. I now have and express the same joy in my grandchildren and the children in my church and community. The older women should express joy and delight in the children and thus be an example of one who does not hinder the children from being drawn to the Lord Jesus.

If the older woman observes a younger woman struggling with depression, anxiety, or resentment towards her children, she should gently come alongside her and help her. What is really in a woman's heart will be shown in how the young mother treats her children. If she is sad and in despair over life, that is the view of life her children will likely embrace. If she is joyful over what the Lord is doing, that is the view of life her children will likely embrace. We cannot save our children from their sin. Only God can. However, we can help the younger mothers to delight in the Lord, express affection and godly delight in their children, and thus draw the children to Him.

So far we have learned that the Titus 2 woman is to teach the younger woman to love her children by teaching her to think loving thoughts, by holding her accountable to be kind and tender-hearted, and by encouraging her to express affection and delight in the children. Now I want to mention one last point –

Teach Them How to Lovingly Administer Godly Discipline

Children are born sinners. Precious as they are, folly is bound in their hearts and it shows forth sometimes several times in one day! Scripture gives us clear instructions –

Foolishness is bound up in the heart of a child;
the rod of discipline will remove it far from him.
Proverbs 22:15

Many young mothers do not know how or when it is appropriate to spank their child. The purpose of this book is not to explain everything I can about spanking. It is to show you the responsibility of the older women to teach and encourage the younger women to appropriately spank their children. (For more information on spanking see Roy Lessin's book, <u>Spanking</u>.)[14]

Often little tips will help a young mother tremendously. These kinds of practical applications frequently mean the difference between godly, loving administration of discipline that brings a child to repentance and cruel, malicious administration of discipline that provokes a child to anger (see Ephesians 6:1-4).

I have found it to be very helpful to tell the mother to spank the child the <u>first</u> time the child disobeys or the mother perceives a sinful attitude in the child. She should train them to obey her the <u>first</u> time she tells them to "stop" (as they are about to run in front of a car). She should not train them to obey <u>after</u> she counts to three or snaps her fingers five times. Usually by the time a mother tells a child three or four times to do something or not do something, the mother is exasperated and speaking in a harsh, angry tone of voice. She may even be yelling at the top of her lungs. Instead, she should instruct the child one time. She should speak in a gentle, normal tone of voice. If the child does not obey or has a sinful attitude, she should calmly spank him. If the mother disciplines the child quickly, she is much less likely to become sinfully angry herself. Instead of provoking her child to anger, she will probably see the fruit of righteousness! The older more mature women should practically help the younger women to love their children by appropriate, godly, loving discipline.

Conclusion

The world does not know how to help young women love their husbands and love their children. Most of what they read about or view on television in regards to loving their husbands could be summed up in the song, "Love Makes the World Go Round." Well, love does not make the world go round, God does. As our Creator, He knows better than we do how a young woman can really love her husband in a righteous, mature, God-honoring way.

Likewise, most of what the young women read about or view on television in regards to loving their children could be summed up in a self-esteem view of the world; that of having their "significance, security and identity needs met." Instead, the Titus 2 women should use the pure, God-breathed Word of God to teach and encourage the younger women. They should be involved in the younger women's lives in an unselfish, personal way. Teaching them to love their husbands and love their children is only the beginning. In the next chapter, we will consider what other qualities a Titus 2 woman teaches the younger woman – to be sensible, to be pure, and to be a worker at home.

Chapter Six

Study Questions

1. What are some possible reasons why the older Christian women are not involved in teaching and encouraging the younger women?

2. Explain what "to love their husbands" means.

3. Write down five examples of *philos* thoughts that you could think towards your husband if you are married. If you are not married, make up examples that a friend could use.

4. Write down four examples of *philos* actions.

5. How does the "one-flesh" bond of love deepen?

6. Explain what "to love their children" means.

7. Give one example of a loving thought a mother could think towards her child for each of the following circumstances:

    A. Her three year old wakes in the middle of the night crying with a sore throat and fever.

    B. Her five year old is slow trying to tie his shoes and his mother is in a hurry.

    C. The budget is really tight and the child needs to go to the doctor. The doctor is expensive.

D. Her two and a half year old screams in anger when told to get in the bed.

8. How does a mother with malice in her heart treat her children?

9. How would you explain to her how she could turn from malice to compassion?

10. List five ways a mother could express affection and delight in her children.

11. What are some practical tips an older woman could give a younger woman regarding spanking?

Chapter Seven

To Be Sensible and Pure

I can just hear my Daddy say, "That kid hasn't got good sense!" And you know what? Sometimes he was talking about me! And you know what else? He was right! Daddy tried valiantly to put some "sense" into me. Through no fault of his own, he did not always succeed. As a result, I grew into a young woman who still lacked what my Daddy called "good sense."

You do not have to look very far to find young women today who (as I was) lack good sense. What my Daddy calls "good sense" the Bible calls "be sensible" (Titus 2:5). Of course, God knew that always being sensible would be a problem for women from the moment Eve sinned. Consequently, He instructed the older women to teach and encourage the younger women to be sensible.

"To be sensible" is the Greek word *sophron*. *Sophron* is a broad term meaning "sound mind, prudent, self-controlled."[15] From this, I thought of three practical applications. The older woman is to teach and encourage the younger woman to:

◆ Have biblical priorities and make wise commitments

◆ Stay within her budget

◆ Face reality

Have Biblical Priorities and Make Wise Commitments

Many of today's young women want it all <u>now</u>. They want a husband and children and an education and a career. Consequently, they may unwisely jeopardize their relationship with their husbands and children (to say nothing of God) to have their way. More than once I have heard of a young mother who is determined to overcome any financial or child-care obstacle in order to attain her career goals. Certainly at best, she is not being prudent.

Prudent is a good old-fashioned word which means "wise." As there are only so many hours in a day, young wives and mothers must decide prudently how to use them. They could benefit from Paul's warning to the Christians in Ephesus to be careful with their time.

> *Therefore be careful how you walk, not as unwise men, but as wise, <u>making the most of your time,</u> because the days are evil. So then do not be foolish, but understand what the will of the Lord is.*
> *Ephesians 5:15-17, emphasis added*

In Psalm 90, Moses saw the wisdom of carefully using whatever days God has allotted for you.

> *So teach us to number our days, that we may present to Thee a heart of wisdom.*
> *Psalm 90:12*

The older I become, the more I think about the time I may have left. If I have (Lord willing) twenty more productive years of service for the Lord, I want to be able to look back on those years and know that by His grace I accomplished His highest purpose. God used that line of reasoning in my life to cause me to quit pursuing a Master's Degree in Religion from a large Christian University and instead to write The Excellent Wife book. From an eternal perspective, which one will have been more important? Obviously, helping women to be godly wives.

It is common for a young Christian wife and mother either to not understand or to rebel against the idea that her primary ministry is to be in the home. She is to serve her husband, children, and also her church. Often her priorities are unwise and unbiblical. She may be very busy but not necessarily doing what the Lord wants her to do. This whole concept is one that should be taught by the older women, exemplified by the older women, and encouraged privately from the older women to the younger women.

It is also important to realize that just because a young woman is doing something for the Lord, it may not necessarily be what the Lord desires for her to do at that time. For example, I have heard of women who have very passionate and tender hearts for the Pro-Life movement. There is no question that working to save babies is a godly pursuit. However, when they neglect their own family and go against the counsel of their husband to pursue rallies all over the country or spend countless hours at the Crisis Pregnancy Center, their priorities become unbiblical. If this kind of ministry is God's will for her, it will still be there when the children are older and she is freer to pursue other things. There is a time for everything in life. Time-consuming ministries outside the home are not usually prudent for a young wife and mother.

You may be wondering if a young wife and mother should do anything outside her home. Certainly, it is not a sin if she does. What is sinful are unbiblical priorities and not being wise about the use of her time and energy.

Recently I spoke to a ladies' class at a church near my home. It was on a Thursday evening. One of the young women asked me about priorities. She has two small children and said, "Today is Thursday and I have been out somewhere every night this week doing something with the church. What do you think?" Well, I think that is too much. Obviously she was frustrated. I recommended that she discuss this with her husband and stop some of her activities. It is much more prudent for her to do fewer things for the Lord, things of high priority such as serving her husband, taking care of her home, and bringing her children up in the "discipline and instruction of the Lord", and to do them well and joyously for Him (Ephesians 6:4, 5:19-20).

Another area the older women can teach and encourage the younger women in is to be sensible with money.

Stay Within Her Budget

When it comes to money and wives...

House and wealth are an inheritance from fathers, but a prudent wife is from the LORD.
Proverbs 19:14

My experience has been that young women do not always know how to make a budget and stay within its parameters. In that case, the older women or perhaps someone in the church should teach them or the young couples how to make a budget. There is also good material and free counsel available through Larry Burkett's ministry, "Christian Financial Concepts."[16] Even though many women do not know how to make an appropriate budget, I have found that a more serious underlying problem is they are not content with what God has given them.

One of the most important influences an older woman can have over a younger woman is to help the younger woman be grateful and content instead of grumbling and complaining. One very powerful passage is I Timothy 6:6-10.

> *But godliness actually is a means of great gain, when accompanied by contentment. For we have brought nothing into the world, so we cannot take anything out of it either. <u>And if we have food and covering, with these we shall be content.</u> But those who want to get rich fall into temptation, and a snare and many foolish and harmful desires which plunge men into ruin and destruction. For the love of money is a root of all sorts of evil, and some by longing for it have wandered away from the faith, and pierced themselves with many a pang.*
>
> *I Timothy 6:6-10, emphasis added*

Instant credit and slick marketing techniques coupled with a young woman's inexperience and sinful heart make it very difficult for her to resist the temptation to purchase beyond her means. And even if she does resist, she may be miserable. It is so easy to be perfectly happy and go shopping only to discover something that you did not even know existed. Now that you have discovered it, you want it.

When I was counseling at the Atlanta Biblical Counseling Center, women would occasionally tell me "When I feel depressed or anxious I go shopping." It was amazing what they bought. Sometimes it was lavish, matching outfits from the new hat for their head down to the new designer shoes for their feet. Other times, it was expensive furniture. Whatever they bought, they felt better for a little while. Ultimately however, they felt guilty (as they should have) and more anxious or depressed trying to figure out how to pay for their new goodies.

In a case like this, the older woman should encourage the younger woman to be grateful and to thank the Lord for what she has and what He is teaching her. Her attitude should be one of "giving thanks (in the name of the Lord Jesus) ... to God the Father" (Colossians 3:17). She should exercise self-control when the money is tight and simply not go shopping or write any checks.

Gratefully staying within her budget is one way a young woman can be sensible in the *sophron* sense. Another way she can be sensible is to . . .

Face Reality

Having a good mind involves facing reality with a hope in God. Philippians 4:8 instructs us to let our minds dwell on "whatever is true." A true thought is one that faces reality. A God-honoring true thought is one that faces reality and expresses a hope in God. For example, instead of thinking "My husband might lose his job. I cannot take the pressure", think "My husband might lose his job, but God is good and He will give us the grace to go through it if it happens." The first thought in this example leaves God out of the picture and is despairing and overwhelming. The second thought is certainly not pleasant but by including God, there is hope instead of despair. Regardless of the difficulty of the circumstances, there is always hope when God is in the picture.

In addition to teaching the younger woman to face reality by thinking rightly, the older woman should have a calming effect on the younger woman. In other words, she should give her hope and turn her to the Lord. Facing a difficult circumstance without hope would add unnecessarily to the younger woman's burden.

Recently, I talked with a young woman who is in a very difficult situation. Some would consider it a crisis. One day at the end of a phone conversation she said, "I always feel better when I talk with you." Why? Because I helped her face what was happening but face it in such a way that she honored the Lord and turned to Him. She felt better, not because she talked to me, but because she turned her thinking from herself to her Lord.

Another way to face reality is to think biblically. Years ago when I was a student nurse I was assigned to a large state psychiatric hospital for one quarter. I met several patients who had delusional beliefs about God. One thought she had given birth to the Christ child. Others thought they were God or the Lord Jesus Christ. They were outwardly religious but inwardly lost. Their minds were not sound. They had (as the world says) "lost their minds."

No one has ever "lost their mind" because they believed God's Word, thought rightly about God, and obeyed Him. Shortly before I became a Christian, I was very emotionally unstable. After I was saved, God began to renew my mind through His Word (Romans 12:1-2). As I read the Bible, prayed, and began to grow in His grace, I became more and more stable every day. God wants us to face reality which includes thinking rightly about Him and ourselves. Godly older women teach and encourage the younger women to face reality.

As I wrote earlier, "to be sensible" is a broad term that encompasses having self-control, being prudent, and having a sound mind. My Daddy talked about having good sense. He tried to help me and now I am trying to help the younger Christian women.

In addition to helping the younger women to be sensible, the older Christian woman is to teach and encourage them to be pure.

To Be Pure

When I became a Christian, I thought I was so holy. Actually, I <u>felt</u> holy. Then the day came when I discovered that thoughts can be sinful. At that point, I learned that I was not nearly as holy as I had previously believed. In fact, I was continuing to sin greatly against God.

The Greek word translated "to be pure" in Titus 2 is *hagnos.* *Hagnos* means to be "free from ceremonial defilement; holy; sacred; chaste; pure; free from sin; and innocent."[17] This word is similar to the word *hagios* which is often translated "holy." [18] This righteous purity is not only outward chastity but also inward freedom from impure thoughts.

Often bondage to sinful lust is thought to be a problem for men but not women. That is not true. Women also may be enticed into the world of fantasies, self-gratification, pornography, and immorality. It all begins with their thoughts.

Pure Thoughts

According to the Scriptures, the heart of man is who he is on the inside. It is what he thinks and what motivates him. There is no secret, hidden, unconscious force making us do things that are not right. We are fully responsible before God for what we think and do. The Lord Jesus Christ was very concerned about the purity of man. He explained that an impure heart comes from what one thinks and then is outwardly manifested.

> *But the things that proceed out of the mouth come from the heart, and those defile the man. For out of the heart come evil thoughts, murders, adulteries, fornications, thefts, false witness, slanders. These are the things which defile the man...*
>
> Matthew 15:18-20

So, it is vitally important that all Christian women repent from any sinful daydreaming, sexual fantasies, or self-gratification. These sinful habits are usually hard to break but certainly not impossible by the grace of God. If she has trained herself to think in a lustful way, she can also train herself by God's grace to stop. When she thinks an impure thought, she must replace it with a God-honoring thought. Certainly, sin does bring a certain amount of momentary pleasure but the ultimate guilt before God is not worth the few moments' fun.

The biblical criteria for pure thoughts is found in Philippians 4:8. "Finally, brethren, whatever is ...pure...let your mind dwell on these things." These are thoughts that do not lead to lust. The greater the bondage to sexual lust, the harder she must work to turn her thoughts to and set her affections on the Lord.

Sometimes asking sexual questions is embarrassing for the older woman and humiliating for the younger woman. The more matter-of-fact the older woman is in asking questions, the easier it will be for the younger woman to open up and talk with her. Obviously, these are very sensitive subjects and should be reserved for a time that is private and after the older woman has developed a good relationship with the younger woman. If the younger woman has a problem, the Titus 2 woman should hold her accountable by asking frequently how she is doing. It would probably help for the older woman to ask the younger woman to write down what she is <u>going to think</u> the next time she is tempted. Perhaps it may be to turn her thoughts to praying for specific people or singing a song that is honoring to the Lord. In addition to thinking godly, pure thoughts, the older woman should teach and encourage the younger woman to avoid situations that might cause her to be tempted.

Make No Provision for the Flesh

The Apostle Paul made it clear that every Christian's actions are to be pure before the Lord. Christians are to turn from their former, lustful way of life.

> *The night is almost gone, and the day is at hand. Let us therefore lay aside the deeds of darkness and put on the armor of light. Let us behave properly as in the day, not in carousing and drunkenness, not in sexual promiscuity and sensuality, not in strife and jealousy. But put on the Lord Jesus Christ, and <u>make no provision for the flesh in regard to its lusts</u>.*
> ***Romans 13:12-14, emphasis added***

For a woman, making no provision for her flesh would include television soap operas, romance novels, pornography, lying in bed, some forms of music, and daydreaming. I knew one young professing Christian wife and mother who not only made provision for her flesh but she also organized her entire life around her "soaps." If she had errands to run or a doctor's appointment, she made sure she was home in time for her television shows. Some mornings she completed her housework in a rush so that nothing would disturb her afternoon programs. She filled her heart (mind) with impure, defiled thoughts. It came as no surprise to me when she divorced her husband for no good reason other than he was not exciting enough for her. No husband could possibly be as exciting as the one a woman could dream up in her mind.

People can also be a provision for the flesh. For instance, a woman involved in a homosexual relationship may have an idolatrous attachment to another woman. In illicit sex, the emotions are inordinate. There is a very strong influence because God "gives them over to degrading passions; for their women exchanged the natural function for that which is unnatural . . ." (Romans 1:26). In addition to helping her cry out to God for mercy to repent, the older woman must also help the younger woman to drastically restructure her life. If she continues to live with or fraternize with her homosexual partner, it is not likely that the younger woman will succeed in breaking the sinful bondage of homosexuality.

It would probably help the younger woman if the older woman expressed a genuine concern for the woman's partner. She might offer to help the partner (if she wants help) or offer to refer her to a pastor or another godly, older woman. Certainly it would be glorifying to God if someone had the opportunity to present to both of them the claims of Jesus Christ (see I Corinthians 6:9-11). Just cutting her off with no concern for her well-being makes it unnecessarily difficult for the young woman and is not merciful.

The young woman may wrongly believe she is responsible for her homosexual lover. Her lover may have said, "You're the only one who loves me. I cannot live without you." Such thinking is simply not true. She may also think, "No one will ever love me the way she did." To that I would recommend the Titus 2 woman reply, "God forbid that anyone would ever love you in such an ungodly way!" Teach her that true, biblical love is love that "rejoices in the truth, it does not rejoice in unrighteousness" (I Corinthians 13:6). It is pure before the Lord and pleasing to Him.

Whether the older woman is helping the homosexual, a teenager having sex with her boyfriend, or a middle-aged woman committing adultery, it is vital that she help them to make no provision for the flesh. If any one of them claim to be a Christian and will not repent, the older woman should bring two or more witnesses with her and biblically confront them (see Matthew 18:15-16). If she still will not repent, it becomes a matter of church discipline. The older woman should go to her pastor and/or elders and ask them to become involved (see Matthew 18:17-18).[19] These are vital steps in the process of the older woman teaching and encouraging (remember this involves warning) the young woman to be pure.

As honoring to the Lord as repenting from impure thoughts and actions is, it is even more honoring if the young woman has remained pure. Even though some testimonies are exciting and it is incredible how God has changed people, those who are innocent and have remained pure before the Lord are a greater trophy of His grace. So, the older woman should teach and encourage the younger women to . . .

Remain Innocent

In Titus 1:15, Paul wrote "to the pure all things are pure." As I think of this, I do not believe this means to be naive. It does, however, mean not to expose yourself to unnecessary impurity. It is one thing to have a definitional understanding of things so that you can protect yourself, your children, and help the younger women; but it is another to read dirty books, look at pornography, and watch soap operas on television.

My good friend Maribeth Standring is a single lady who has kept herself pure. In the last few years she has become involved in a counseling ministry to younger Christian women where she works. Some of them were married or getting married, others were homosexuals. They each had explicit questions about sex. In order to give them clear biblical guidance, Maribeth had to understand better what the younger women were talking about. Maribeth would call me and ask me. I gave her enough information so that she could give them godly counsel. I did not, however, give her sordid sensual details that might tempt her to think wrongly. She had to overcome her embarrassment as well as lack of knowledge but she did not have to lose her purity.

Summary

"Teaching them to be pure" is a huge challenge in our Corinthian culture. Sex is a god in America. God intended it to be wonderful, fun, and pure. Sinful man has perverted it to something dirty, sinful, and wicked. The older women <u>must</u> teach the younger women, hold them accountable, protect them, and if the younger woman has a sexual moral failure, exhort her to repent.

Chapter Conclusion

This chapter explained what it means to teach and encourage the younger women to be sensible and pure. For each of these, we considered three practical applications showing <u>what</u> it is the Titus 2 woman is to teach. The older woman should help the younger women to be sensible by adhering to biblical priorities through making wise commitments, by staying within her budget, and by facing reality. The older woman should also help the younger women to be pure by thinking pure thoughts, making no provision for the flesh, and remaining innocent.

In the next chapter, we will learn <u>how</u> the Titus 2 Woman can teach and encourage the younger woman to be a worker at home and to be kind.

Chapter Seven

Study Questions

1. What does the Greek word *sophron* mean?

2. List the three practical applications in chapter seven that the older woman could use to teach and encourage the younger woman "to be sensible."

3. Can you think of any others?

4. What should be the priorities of a wife and mother? What is her primary ministry?

5. What is likely a more serious underlying problem regarding money than not knowing how to make a budget?

6. What is a good Scripture passage to teach to a younger woman who is not content with what she has?

7. Explain in detail what you would say to a young woman who is distraught and says, "My husband is ill. He might have cancer. If he does, I can't stand it. I can't take the pressure!"

8. List four or five Scriptures that you might use in teaching and encouraging other woman to be pure.

9. Write down what could be "provisions for the flesh" in your own life as well as in the lives of others.

10. How might an older woman keep herself pure and yet understand enough about impurity to help a younger woman?

11. What about your thoughts and actions? Are they pure before the Lord or are you ashamed when you realize that God knows all your thoughts and actions. Is there an impurity from which you need to turn? Begin by confessing your sin to God. (See I John 1:9). Next, plan how not to make provision for your flesh. If needed, ask another godly woman to hold you accountable.

Chapter Eight

To Be A Worker At Home and To Be Kind

One of the most frequent questions I am asked is "Is it all right for a Christian woman to work outside the home?" I dread this question because no matter how I reply, someone will be upset with me. My answer has changed over the last fifteen years. As a new Christian, I did not really have an opinion one way or the other. There were too many other biblical issues that I was trying to comprehend. Later, I believed that no Christian woman regardless of her age or her circumstances should ever work outside the home. Now I have come to understand that God is more concerned about a woman's heart than He is outward conformity to an absolute rule. The point is, for the most part, she should not work outside of the home. She should be content to be at home and serve her family and make material sacrifices when necessary. However, if her heart is pure before Him and her motive is to glorify God, it is wrong for me to be absolutely dogmatic about the younger women never working for any reason. See, I told you someone would be upset!

The phrase "worker at home" in Titus 2:5 is the Greek word *oikouros*. This a compound word which comes from two root words – *oikos* which means "a dwelling, a home, or a household" and *ergon* which means "to work or be employed."[20] I have tried and cannot think of any better way to explain what I believe about women working than what I wrote in The Excellent Wife book.[21]

The biblical concept of a "worker at home" is not a popular one today, but I do believe that God intended for the women, especially the younger women, to stay home and do a good job of caring for their homes and for their families. A wife who is gone with too many activities or work does not have the time or energy to keep her home as it should be kept.

If a wife is working or is thinking of returning to work, she should examine her motives. What is it she really wants? What is her heart set on? Is it to avoid becoming a "non-person?" Is it more material things? Is it wanting to be out from under the demands of child care? Is it to relieve her husband from his responsibility to work? None of these motives are for the glory of God. They are self-serving and sinful. Godly motives would be "learning to be content" (Philippians 4:11), gratitude to the Lord for what she does have (I Thessalonians 5:18), and "whatever you do in thought, word, and deed, do all for the glory of God" (I Corinthians 10:31). Staying at home and organizing a clean, well run household is a major biblical emphasis in the God-given ministry of the wife.

You may be thinking, "That's all well and good, but what about the couple who is in debt?" A couple who is in so much debt that the wife may have to work should consider making sacrifices in order to live within their budget while systematically working towards debt reduction. In other words, they would work towards her quitting work and staying home. Many times, if a couple did an honest appraisal of the wife's income, and looked at how much they spent on transportation, child care, taxes, clothing, lunches out, dinners out, and increased grocery bills due to buying prepared foods, the couple would likely see that they are actually losing money. How much wiser might it be for her to stay home and care for her family! Even if it means her husband getting an additional temporary part-time job for paying off the debts, he still is likely to have more left over energy than he currently does because his wife would be home helping him by organizing the family's life, clothes, food, etc.

What if a husband instructs a wife to work? Is she to be submissive? Yes, unless the wife can show him that she would be sinning by working. It would be sinful for her to financially support her husband so that he could be irresponsible or lazy. Instead, she should take advantage of the biblical resources God has given to protect her.[22] Although not a sin, it may be wise not to work and place children in child care if the children are susceptible to repeated illnesses from exposure to the other children in the day care center. Certainly, it is a sin if through surrogate child care, the children are not being brought up in the "discipline and instruction of the Lord" (Ephesians 6:4).

One young mother that I counseled showed her husband with what she could earn she would ultimately lose money by working. She did, however, come up with a creative alternative and worked two to three mornings a week cleaning houses while the children were at school. Later, she worked part-time for her husband out of their home as he started a new business. This option worked better because she could still run her home and take care of her children.

What if the husband becomes ill or dies? In some cases, I believe her church has a responsibility to help her be able to stay home with her children (see I Timothy 5:1-6). If the church will not, she may have to seek employment either from her home or outside of her home.

Unless providentially hindered by God, it is the wife's responsibility to be a "worker at home" and maintain an orderly and organized home. It does not mean that her husband and children cannot help, but she sets the tone. Chaos and disorder create tension and contention. It drains her of the needed energy to work on her relationship with her husband and children. A wife should make it her business to find out how to keep an orderly and clean home and stay organized with her grocery shopping and meals. There are many good books on the market or in the library that are very helpful, and if this area in her life is out of control, she should seek the resources to change.

Even though being a "worker at home" is not a popular idea, it should be a joy for each Christian wife and mother. She is to work (*ergon*) in her home. Pastor John MacArthur explains *ergon* this way --

Ergon does not simply refer to labor in general; it often refers to a particular job or employment. It is the word Jesus used when He said, "My food is to do the will of Him who sent Me, and to accomplish His <u>work</u>" (John 4:34, emphasis added). Our Lord focused His entire life on fulfilling God's will. In a similar fashion, a wife is to focus her life on the home. God has designed the family to be her sphere of responsibility. That doesn't mean she should spend twenty-four hours a day there, however. The woman in Proverbs

31 left her home when she needed to buy a field or when she needed supplies, yet even those trips benefited her family. She poured her life into her family – she woke up early and went to bed late for the sake of those in it.

Notice that Paul didn't make any effort to elaborate on what he meant by "workers at home." That's because his readers were completely familiar with the term. The Mishna, an ancient codification of Jewish law and tradition, gives us some insight into what life was like for a wife in Paul's day. She was expected to grind flour, bake, launder, cook, nurse her children, make the beds, spin wool, prepare the children for school, and accompany them to school to ensure their arrival. While many women worked with their husbands in the field or in a trade, the husband still held the responsibility to provide food and clothing. If any women worked apart from their husbands in the marketplace or at a trade, they were considered a disgrace. A wife could, however, work at crafts or horticulture in the home and sell the fruits of her labor. Profits from her endeavors could then be used either to supplement her husband's income or provide her with some spending money. In addition to household work, wives were responsible for hospitality and the care of guests, and to be active in charitable work. The Jewish laws were clear: the woman's priority was in the home. She was to take care of all the needs of her home, her children, her husband, strangers, the poor and needy, and guests. The wife who faithfully discharged her responsibilities was held in high regard in her family, in the synagogue, and in the community. [23]

Now that we have considered what it means to be a "worker at home," I want to turn our thought to the purpose of this chapter which is <u>what</u> the Titus 2 Woman is to teach the younger woman regarding working at home. There are at least three things: exhort them to work hard and not be lazy, give them tips on how to be organized, and help them to anticipate their family's needs.

Exhort Them to Work Hard and Not be Lazy

She looks well to the ways of her household and does not eat the bread of idleness.
Proverbs 31:27

A godly wife works hard and is not lazy. She should stay home enough to get her work done. I have heard of women who pride themselves on being "night people." That means they have trouble getting up in the mornings because they come alive late at night. They may stay up to all hours reading, watching television, or pursuing some sort of interest. The next morning they are too tired to get up and care for their family. Children are left to fend for themselves. Husbands, too.

These women are not "night people." They are lazy and selfish. Who would not rather stay up late to do whatever they pleased and sleep late the next day? Lazy people are often busy, but they are not busy doing the work that God has given them to do. They are incredibly self-indulgent. The older, more mature women in the church should lovingly but firmly confront these young Christian mothers and exhort them not to be selfish, but to consider their families as "more important than themselves" (Philippians 2:3).

Once a young wife begins getting up earlier than her children and her husband, she will cease to be a "night person." She will be tired at night and go to bed at a reasonable hour so she will be there to serve her family the next morning. She will be like the Excellent Wife in Proverbs 31:15 who "rises also while it is still night and gives food to her household."

In addition to exhorting the younger women to work hard and not be lazy, the Titus 2 Woman should know how to be organized herself and give the younger women helpful hints.

Give Tips on How to be Organized

Simple tips can revolutionize a younger woman's life. Here are some examples.

PRACTICAL TIPS ON HOW TO BE ORGANIZED
1. Make a list of all your work to be done that day.
2. Place the items on the list in order of priority from the one you least desire to do down to the one that you like to do the most. Do the hardest ones or the ones you least desire to do first.
3. With the exception of beginning a load of laundry, completely finish one task before you go on to another.
4. If you have an item in your hand, do not put it down unless you are putting it where it belongs. This will save untold hours of hunting for things. It will also keep you from feeling overwhelmed. If your house is two-story, place the items to go upstairs in a basket at the bottom of the steps. The next time you go upstairs, take the basket and put those items away.

5. As you see that you are running low on food, cleaning supplies, or other items, write the item down on a conveniently placed list.

6. Think about birthday cards and other cards or presents you will need for the upcoming month. Purchase them at one time near the end of the previous month. Keep one or two sympathy, thank you, and birthday cards on hand that you may use if needed.

7. When you purchase a gift, wrap it either as soon as you get home or at least the day before you need it. Then, it will be ready and save a last minute rush.

8. Get up earlier than the rest of the family and get dressed and ready for the day. The entire day will be much less frantic.

9. Purchase a file cabinet or a box with folders. Mark the folders with categories you will use, and file papers for future use. Some categories you might find useful are medical information, important business papers, correspondence, etc.

One of the young women that I disciple in a Titus 2 fashion is Kimberley. Kimberley is a good example of someone who is organized and works hard. She works diligently to plan meals, grocery shop, and cook.

Kimberley is currently teaching a ladies' Bible study class to several younger wives. One day, they asked Kimberley to teach them how to plan menus and to shop for groceries. She replied, "OK. Be here Saturday at 8:00 A.M. and I will take you shopping." Although there were audible moans and groans due to the earliness of the hour, her class agreed to be there. They, too, wanted to learn from Kimberley and become women who "looked well to the ways of their households" (Proverbs 31:27).

In addition to exhorting the younger woman to work hard and not be lazy and also giving her tips on how to be organized, the Titus 2 Woman should help her...

Anticipate Her Family's Needs

WAYS TO ANTICIPATE HER FAMILY'S NEEDS
1. Always have at least one easy, quick meal available or prepared in the freezer in the event she is providentially hindered from cooking.
2. Keep up with the ironing on a weekly basis.
3. Make sure her husband has clean underwear in his drawer.
4. Plan ahead for children's clothes purchases. For example, she could purchase very nice quality clothing on close-out at the end of season clearance sale if she takes into consideration what size her child will be the following season.
5. If you are sewing an item to be completed by a particular date, start early so you can take your time and do a good job.
6. Keep enough food on hand to be able to prepare nutritious meals and snacks on time.
7. Post a list of future errands such as "Items needed from the drug store." Encourage family members to record their needs as they arise.

My friend, Carol, is a sterling example of a woman who anticipates her family's needs. She irons their clothes as she takes them out of the dryer! I have never met anyone quite like this, but Carol's husband always has a clean, ironed shirt hanging in his closet. Also, she is not unnecessarily flustered trying to find herself something to wear at the last minute.

Like Carol, the Christian woman should be especially skilled in homemaking. Being a "worker at home" is almost a lost art in our culture. Instead of being lost, however, the Titus 2 Woman should be leading the way.

As a Titus 2 Woman teaches and encourages the younger woman to care for her family and home properly, she should also teach and encourage her to set the proper tone in the home. The proper tone begins with being kind.

Teach Her to be Kind

She opens her mouth in wisdom and the teaching of kindness is on her tongue.
Proverbs 31:26

The Greek word for kind is *agathos*. It means to be "generous, good, or kind."[24] We get our beautiful English name Agatha from *agathos*. A woman's goodness, generosity, and kindness should be expressed in performing kind and generous deeds as well as speaking in a gentle tone of voice. The Titus 2 Woman is to show *agathos* by personal example.

Show by Example How to do Kind Deeds

The Titus 2 woman should show by her example how to do kind deeds. Kind deeds are what makes her a beautiful woman, not her physical appearance.

> *Likewise, I want women to adorn themselves with proper clothing, modestly and discreetly, not with braided hair and gold or pearls or costly garments; but rather by means of good (agathos) works, as befits women making a claim to godliness.*
>
> *I Timothy 2:9-10,*
> *emphasis and adaptation added*

Several months ago my pastor, John Crotts, called and asked me to take an elderly lady in our community to her doctor's appointment scheduled for the following day. Mrs. S. had telephoned our church requesting help because one of our members had told her to call if she ever needed us. I cheerfully told John, "I will be glad to take care of it."

My plan was to ask someone else to do this good deed. After several attempts to find someone, it became apparent that the good deed doer was me! As I came to realize that I was stuck with this deed, my cheerfulness began to wane.

By the time I faced the fact that no one else was available, I began to resent this uninvited intrusion on my time. In spite of my resentment, I telephoned Mrs. S. and was very nice to her as I explained I would take her to the doctor the next day. She sounded delightful over the phone and very appreciative. I outwardly did what was right, but in my heart I continued to resent the intrusion into my life.

The next morning, I continued to struggle with a sinful attitude. Finally, I could bear it no longer and I asked God to forgive me. I thanked Him for the opportunity, and I began to look forward to doing this good deed.

A little while later, I received a phone call from the woman who usually accompanied this dear lady to the doctor. She said, "I have been out of town. That is why Mrs. S. has been unable to contact me. I appreciate your offer but if you don't mind, I would rather take her myself." Of course, she did not have to twist my arm!

As I thought about how very wicked and selfish I had been over the entire episode and especially how the Lord had known all along I would not even have to go, I was deeply ashamed and grieved over my sin. As I should have joyfully helped Mrs. S., so should the Titus 2 Woman <u>joyfully</u> perform good deeds.

In addition to being an example to the younger woman, the Titus 2 Woman should help the younger women to speak with kind words.

Help Them Express Kindness by their Words

There are many verses in the Bible that convict me every time I read them. One such verse is Proverbs 31:26. The excellent wife "opens her mouth in wisdom and the teaching of kindness is on her tongue."

Kind words are sympathetic, compassionate, and biblically loving. A kind woman is apt to say something like, "I know this must be hard for you. Is there anything I can do to make it easier?" or "I'm so sorry that this is hard. Let me help you." Thus, she is kind when she opens her mouth.

The Titus 2 Woman is not only kind in her words, but she is also kind in her tone of voice.

Emphasize that a Gentle Tone of Voice is Kind

Many women habitually speak in a sharp, harsh, or sarcastic tone of voice. Thus, they negate any kindness that may have been in their words or actions. Their words are anything but "sweet to the soul and healing to the bones" (Proverbs 16:24). They have not yet taught their mouth how to speak (Proverbs 16:23).

The only way such a woman will break her sinful habit of speaking in a harsh tone is to put off the wrong tone by God's grace through replacing it with a gentle tone. Each time she is too harsh or sharp, she should think about not only <u>what</u> she should have said but also <u>how</u> she should have said it. Then she should practice the correct way aloud. Not only that, but she should go back to the person she has offended and say, "When I spoke to you earlier and said, . . . I should not have said it in that way. What I should have said is, . . ." Eventually, with God's help, she will become a woman who truly has the "teaching of kindness on her tongue" (Proverbs 31:26).

Summary of Teaching Her to be Kind

Being kind encompasses generosity, compassion, and kind deeds. It is shown in practical ways by doing kind deeds joyfully, expressing kind and compassionate words, and speaking those words in a kind and gentle tone of voice. Being kind is one of the hallmarks of being a godly woman. The Titus 2 Woman should do everything she can to help the younger woman adorn herself with true beauty – good deeds done from a kind heart.

Chapter Conclusion

This chapter explains practical ways the Titus 2 Woman can teach and encourage the younger woman to be a "worker at home" and to be kind. These two instructions are the fifth and sixth in a list of seven instructions for the older women to teach the younger women.

In the next chapter, we will cover the seventh (and last) instruction. This one is probably the most controversial and misunderstood of them all – Teach the younger women to be "subject to their own husbands" . . . (Titus 2:5).

Chapter Eight

Study Questions

1. Give some examples of sinful motives when a Christian woman is considering going to work.

2. What are godly motives regarding work?

3. Explain what the word *ergon* means. See the quote in chapter eight from John MacArthur regarding *ergon*.

4. Do you consider yourself to be a hard worker and well organized? If not, what could you do differently? Be very specific.

5. How would you describe words that are kind?

6. Look up the following verses and write down what you learn about how we are to speak:

   A. Proverbs 16:21

   B. Proverbs 22:11

C. Ecclesiastes 5:6

D. Colossians 3:8

E. Colossians 4:6

F. I Timothy 4:12

G. Psalm 34:13

H. Ephesians 4:~~15~~ 14 -15

I. Ephesians 5:19 - 20

J.   Matthew 12:34-36

K. Luke 6:45

L. Proverbs 16:24

M. Proverbs 31:26

7.   After reading the previous verses on speech, what is your prayer?

Chapter Nine

To Be Subject To Her Own Husband

For a wife to be biblically under the authority of her husband is the heart of God for the Christian wife. The New Testament gives the same command to wives in four separate places. Each time the command is given, it is accompanied by God's reason to obey.

1. "Wives, be subject to your own husband, <u>as to the Lord</u>" (Ephesians 5:22, emphasis added).

2. "Wives, be subject to your husbands, <u>as is fitting in the Lord</u>" (Colossians 3:18, emphasis added).

3. "Older women likewise are to . . . teach what is good that they may encourage the young women to . . . (be) subject to their own husbands, <u>that the Word of God may not be dishonored</u>" (Titus 2:3-5, emphasis added).

4. "For in this way in former times the holy women also, who hoped in God, used to adorn themselves, being submissive to their own husbands. Thus Sarah obeyed Abraham, calling him lord, and you have become her children if you <u>do what is right</u> without being frightened by any fear" (I Peter 3:5-6, emphasis added).

There really is no justifiable way (cultural or otherwise) to get around the fact that the wife is to be submissive to her husband. If a wife is going to be in God's will, she must be rightfully, biblically submissive. Because this topic is so maligned in the world and in the church, the Titus 2 Woman needs to be especially skilled at helping the younger women do what is right. She should begin with teaching the younger women the doctrine of biblical submission.

Teach Her the Doctrine of Biblical Submission

"Being subject to" is the Greek word *hupotasso*. This word is comprised of two Greek words – *hupo* ("to be under") and *tasso* ("to draw up in order, to arrange, to designate").[25] This word is a military term and it means to be ranked under in military order. For example, in the Army the General is ranked over the Captain, the Captain over the Lieutenant, the Lieutenant over the Sergeant, etc. Thus, the wife is ranked under her husband regarding authority in the home and in their marriage.

Hupotasso means the wife is to be submissive to her husband in all things (big and little) unless her husband asks her to sin. If her husband wants her to lie for him or cover up his sin, for example, he is asking her to sin. If he wants to bring pornography into their bedroom, he is asking her to sin. Otherwise, if it is not a sin issue, she is to graciously obey. According to the verses we just looked at earlier, that is God's will for her.

In addition to teaching the younger woman what submission means, the older woman should explain clearly God's view of authority.

Teach Her about God's Authority Structure in the Home

God sovereignly ordained authority in the home, so there would not be chaos but harmony. The biblically submissive role is how God chose for the wife to glorify Him. He also intended to protect the wife and the children through the husband's leadership.

> *For the husband is the head of the wife, as Christ also is the head of the church, He Himself being the Savior of the body.*
>
> *Ephesians 5:23*

The husband is given authority in the home but an important consideration is that his authority is not absolute. Only God has absolute authority. So, if a husband asks his wife to sin, then she must (as Peter did in the book of Acts) "obey God rather than man" (Acts 5:29). Think of it this way, if the Lieutenant has received conflicting orders from his Captain and his General, which one should he obey? Of course, he should obey the General's command. In the same way, God's commands override any sinful command that a husband might give.

I want to elaborate on this point because there is a wrong view of authority taught by some pastors and some Christian women. These are people whom I consider to be godly and who love the Lord very much. However, they are misinterpreting I Peter 3:5-6.

For in this way in former times the holy women also, who hoped in God, used to adorn themselves, being submissive to their own husband. Thus Sarah obeyed Abraham, calling him lord, and you have become her children if you do what is right without being frightened by any fear.

Their misinterpretation is explained something like this. In the book of Genesis, Abraham asked Sarah to lie for him and say, "I am his sister." She was to deceptively leave out the information that she was also his wife! Thus, their conclusion is that every wife is supposed to obey her husband no matter what her husband has asked her to do. Then she will be like Sarah and do "what is right" by obeying. God will consequently hold her husband accountable for any sin, and she will be like a godly woman of old.

The problem with this interpretation is that Peter is not telling a wife to sin for her husband. There are, in fact, many verses that make it clear we are each responsible for our individual sin. The fact is that in the book of Genesis, Sarah was sinning as was Abraham. In spite of their sin, God blessed them and rescued them anyway. How much better it would have been if Abraham and Sarah had trusted God in the first place to protect them and keep His promises!

What Peter is saying in this passage is that Sarah (in general) had a pattern in her life of submission. Peter is not saying to obey if the husband asks his wife to sin. To do so would be inconsistent with the character of God and a violation of a multitude of other Scriptures. Peter is not saying that all Sarah did was right any more than all King David did was right. Yet, King David was a man after God's own heart. We too are to be people after God's own heart, but not emulate David's sin.

Teach Her that Submission does Not Mean the Wife is Inferior

Some teach what I call a "doormat" view of submission. The impression this view gives is that somehow the man is superior to and better than the woman. The clear teaching of Scripture, however, is contrary to the "doormat" view.

For there is no partiality with God.

Romans 2:11

There is neither Jew nor Greek, there is neither slave nor free man, there is neither male nor female; for you are all one in Christ Jesus.

Galatians 3:28

You husbands likewise, live with your wives in an understanding way, as with a weaker vessel, since she is a woman; and grant her honor as a fellow heir of the grace of life, so that your prayers may not be hindered.

I Peter 3:7

Some wives are more gifted than their husbands in intellect or talent. Some are better at balancing the checkbook. Some are more godly. But regardless, the wife is still to submit herself to her husband's authority in a gracious manner. The husband may wisely choose to delegate a certain responsibility to her, but he is still the one with the God-given authority. Just as Christ is not inferior to the Father, she is not inferior to her husband. But like the Lord Jesus has a different role than God the Father, she has a different role than her husband. (See I Corinthians 11:3.) The young woman needs to be taught this concept so that she will be less likely to react wrongly to what the Bible teaches about submission.

Teach her How to Make an Appropriate Appeal

Another concept the Titus 2 Woman should teach the younger woman is how to make an appropriate appeal. Just because the woman is to be submissive does not mean that she should not have an opinion or request that her husband change his mind. If she desires to appeal one of his decisions (in a case where he is not asking her to sin), she should begin with something like "Would you consider . . .?"

Her husband would then realize right away that she is not demanding her way, but nicely making a request. She should end her appeal with something like ". . . but whatever you decide, I will do." Then she should <u>do</u> whatever he decides with a cheerful attitude realizing that it is the Lord Jesus she is ultimately serving. Her husband's answer (unless he is asking her to sin) is God's will for her at that time. God alone has the right to determine how a wife may best glorify Him at each particular moment. The Titus 2 Woman should help the younger woman understand that she should be more concerned about glorifying God than having her own way.

In addition to teaching the younger woman doctrine regarding submission, the Titus 2 Woman should be a model to the younger woman of a biblically, submissive wife.

Be A Model of Biblical Submission

It goes without saying that a Titus 2 Woman must live <u>her</u> life in accordance with God's holy standard. If she does not, she is a hypocrite and no one is likely to be rightly influenced by her. The Titus 2 Woman who is married should have the attitude of being joyfully, biblically submissive to her husband. She should thus be serving the Lord with gladness like the Psalmist in Psalm 100:2. She should also learn to give biblical counsel on how to be submissive yet righteously respond if her husband is sinning.

Give Biblical Counsel if the Younger Woman's Husband is Sinning

It is a common occurrence for a younger Christian woman to privately ask an older Christian woman for advice regarding her husband's sin. The older woman may be shocked or even appalled at what she learns from the younger woman. Therefore, it is important that the Titus 2 Woman not overreact and unnecessarily embarrass the younger woman. Instead, she must maintain a biblical perspective on sin. Sin is evil and bad, but by God's grace there is nothing of which the younger woman or her husband cannot repent. There is always hope in God, and the older woman should offer that hope to the younger woman.

In the process of helping the younger woman, the Titus 2 Woman should hear enough to give accurate biblical counsel but not unnecessarily gossip about and slander the young husband. The guideline is to listen to enough information to give sound biblical advice. If the younger woman does not follow through by obeying God's Word and subsequently wants to continue talking about her husband, the Titus 2 Woman should no longer listen but exhort the younger woman to do what is right. In the process of giving biblical counsel, there are at least three things to remember.

1. Counsel the younger woman not to return evil for evil but good for evil.

   Never pay back evil for evil to anyone. Respect what is right in the sight of all men. If possible, so far as it depends on you, be at peace with all men. Never take your own revenge, beloved, but leave room for the wrath of God, for it is written "Vengeance is mine, I will repay," says the LORD. "But if your enemy (or husband) is hungry, feed him, and if he is thirsty, give him a drink; for in so doing you will heap burning coals upon his head." Do not be overcome by evil, but overcome evil with good."

   Romans 12:17-21,
   adaptation and emphasis added

   Every time her husband sins against her, she should retaliate with a blessing instead. She can prepare his favorite meal, pray for him, or think a kind and tender-hearted thought such as "I know he is tired. I wonder what I can do to help him?" As she returns good instead of evil, she will greatly honor the Lord, show direct obedience to His Word, and be much less likely to struggle with sinful bitterness. God will also use her obedience to put added pressure on her husband to repent.

2. Counsel the younger woman to give her husband (if it is appropriate) a biblical reproof. She should go to her husband with his sin, not talk about him to others. If she does not respond biblically, she is likely to become deeply embittered. The guidelines for giving a reproof are in Matthew 18:15-18 and Galatians 6:1. Her reproof should be done gently and with love. Her motive should be to restore him

to a right relationship with God. If he is a Christian, she should use Scripture to back up the reproof. If he is not a Christian, she should appeal to his conscience to do what is right.

I want to make it very clear that I am not talking about "nailing" him every time he steps the slightest bit out of line. But when a wife observes what she believes to be a pattern of sin in her husband's life and he has not responded to her appeals, she has a biblical responsibility to pursue the matter further. There is no Scriptural limit on which sins she should reprove him for and which ones she should not. Whether it is adultery or chronic laziness and irresponsibility, the wife is to reprove her husband in love. If he does not repent and he is a Christian, she is to bring other witnesses into the matter (Matthew 18:16).

3. Teach the younger wife how to "not answer a fool according to his folly" (Proverbs 26:4-5). The best way to explain this is to give an example. Suppose a husband is irresponsible and selfish with money. His wife has made appeals and yet he persists in what she believes to be a clear pattern of sin. She lovingly reproves him and asks him to repent. Instead of agreeing that she is right, he explodes in sinful anger, "You don't care about me. You don't want me to have any fun!!" Rather than defend herself against his manipulative accusations, she should "give the fool the answer he deserves" (Proverbs 26:5). She should **calmly, gently** say something like, "Sweetheart, as a Christian, your responsibility is to talk to me with a kind tone of voice and to repent of your selfishness."

In counseling/discipling the younger woman, encourage her to take full advantage of all the resources God has given to protect her when her husband is sinning. For much more detailed information about these resources, see Chapter Fourteen in The Excellent Wife book.[26]

As the Titus 2 Woman learns how to teach and encourage the younger woman to be subject to her husband, she may encounter one of two biblically wrong views about submission. One is the "mutual submission only" view and the other is the "win him without a word" view.

Unbiblical Teaching about Submission

1. The "mutual submission only" view.

Many today teach an unbiblical view of submission which I will refer to as the "mutual submission only" view. Their belief is based on Ephesians 5:21 which states, ". . . and be subject to one another in the fear of Christ." They say that this is a general command to all Christians. They also say that the next verse which instructs wives to be submissive to their husbands no longer applies as that was a cultural practice in Paul's day. Only the mutual submission still applies today. John Piper and Wayne Grudem, in their book Recovering Biblical Manhood and Womanhood, give a plausible explanation as to why the mutual submission view is not what the Apostle Paul intended. They say . . .

. . . (Ephesians 5:21) does not teach mutual submission at all, but rather teaches that we should all be subject to those whom God has put in authority over us – such as husbands, parents, or employers. In this way, Ephesians 5:21 would be paraphrased, "being subject to one another (that is, *to some others*), in the fear of Christ."

The primary argument for this . . . view is the word *hupotasso* itself. Although many people have claimed that the word can mean "be thoughtful and considerate; act in love" (toward another), it is doubtful if a first-century Greek speaker would have understood it that way, for the term always implies a relationship of submission to an authority. It is used elsewhere in the New Testament of the submission of Jesus to the authority of His parents (Luke 2:51), of demons being subject to the disciples (Luke 10:17, clearly the meaning "act in love, be considerate" cannot fit here);. . . of the universe being subject to Christ (I Corinthians 15:27). . . None of these relationships is ever reversed; that is, husbands are never told to be subject (*hupotasso*) to wives, parents to the child, disciples to demons, etc. . .

Therefore it seems to be a misunderstanding of Ephesians 5:21 to say that it implies mutual submission. Even in Ephesians 5:22-24, wives are not to be subject to everyone or to all husbands, but to "their *own* husbands" – the "submission" Paul has in mind is not a general kind of thoughtfulness toward others, but a specific submission to a higher authority. . .

The reason the mutual submission interpretation is so common is that interpreters *assume* that the Greek pronoun *allelous* ("one another") must be completely reciprocal (that is must mean "everyone to everyone"). . . that is not the case in all of its uses, and it certainly does not have to take that meaning. There are many cases where it rather means "some to others;" for example, in Revelation 6:4, "so that men should slay *one another* means "so that *some* would kill *others*" (not "so that every person would kill every other person," or "so that those people being killed would mutually kill those who were killing them," which would make no sense); in Galatians 6:2, "Bear *one another's* burdens" means not "everyone should exchange burdens with everyone else," but "*some* who are more able should help bear the burdens of *others* who are less able". . .

Therefore, according to this . . . interpretation, it would seem best to say that it is not mutual submission but submission to appropriate authorities that Paul is commanding in Ephesians 5:21.[27]

In addition to a wrong interpretation of the Greek in Ephesians 5, the "mutual submission only" view is common today because of the humanist influence in our society. John MacArthur explains it well.

For the past several hundred years western society has been bombarded with the humanistic, egalitarian, sexless, classless philosophy that was the dominant force behind the French Revolution. The blurring and even total removal of all human distinctions continues to be masterminded by Satan so as to undermine legitimate, God-ordained authority in every realm of human activity – in government, the family, the school, and even in the church. We find ourselves victimized by the godless, atheistic concepts of man's supreme independence from every external law and authority. The philosophy is self-destructive, because no group of people can live in orderliness and productivity if each person is bent on doing his own will.

Sadly, much of the church has fallen prey to this humanistic philosophy and is now willing to recognize the ordination of homosexuals, women, and others whom God's Word specifically disqualifies from church leadership. It is usually argued that biblical teaching contrary to egalitarianism was inserted by biased editors, scribes, prophets, or apostles. And the church is reaping the whirlwind of confusion, disorder, immorality, and apostasy that such qualification of God's Word always spawns. Many Bible interpreters function on the basis of a hermeneutic that is guided by contemporary humanistic philosophy rather than the absolute authority of Scripture as God's inerrant Word.

Peter taught exactly the same truth as Paul in regard to the relationship of husbands and wives, "You wives, be submissive (also from *hupotasso*) to your own husband" (I Peter 3:1). The idea is not that of subservience or servility, but of willingly functioning under the husband's leadership.[28]

Another reason the "mutual submission only" view is not correct is because in Ephesians 5:24 the wives are told to be subject to their husbands as "the church is subject to Christ..." Since there will never be a time that the church is not to be subject to Christ, there will never be a time on this earth when wives are not to be submissive to their husbands. This is not a cultural issue. It is a God-ordained authority issue.

2. The "win him without a word" view.

This view is based on I Peter 3:1-2.

> *In the same way, you wives, be submissive to your own husbands so that even if any of them are disobedient to the word, they may be <u>won without a word</u> by the behavior of their wives, as they observe your chaste and respectful behavior.*
>
> *I Peter 3:1-2, emphasis added*

Some believe that a wife is either never to <u>reprove</u> (tell him what he is doing wrong) her husband (thus win him without a word) or she is to reprove him (and possibly bring witnesses and the church into the matter) only under extreme circumstances such as adultery or wife-beating. Is that what Peter is saying? Let us think through these verses together.

In the same way (our example is the Lord Jesus Christ and His submission to the will of the Father. He suffered unjustly at times and the godly, submissive wife will too at times), **you wives, be submissive to your own husbands** (here is a general command for all wives whether they are married to believers or unbelievers to be submissive to their husbands) **so that even if any of them are disobedient to the word, they may be won without a word by the behavior of their wives, as they observe your chaste and respectful behavior.** (This side note tacked onto the general command to be submissive is about evangelizing – "may be won" -- unsaved husbands – "those who are disobedient to the word." We know the phrase "those who are disobedient to the word" refers to unbelievers because Peter uses the same phrase – "those who are disobedient to the word" – in I Peter 2:7-8 to describe unbelievers who reject the cornerstone, the Lord Jesus Christ. Peter has not mentioned one word about reproof. His point is winning unsaved husbands. Wives are not to stuff gospel tracts in their pillows or

preach to them but win them by their godly, respectful behavior.)

I Peter 3:1-2, explanation added

Peter is saying be submissive and have a godly attitude. Peter
is not saying – "don't say a word to your husband no matter
what he does." Professor D. Edmond Hiebert in his commentary, 1 Peter, explains I Peter 3:1-2 the following way.

Peter taught that it is the duty of the Christian wife
to submit to the authority of her husband whether or
not he is saved. Her submission acquires a saving significance if the husband is not a Christian: "so that, if
any of them do not believe the word, they may be won
over without talk by the behavior of their wives." The
purpose clause, "so that" (*bina*), "in order that," indicates that under undesirable conditions, her submission assumes an evangelistic function. Though Peter
gave no absolute assurance that such a husband would
be saved, he extended that hope as a real possibility.
"If" (*kai ei*), "if also," shows that not all Christian wives
face that distressing situation, but the conditional con-
struction indicates that many of them do. According
to Peter, such a situation was not the result of a Christian woman marrying an unbeliever; it was the result
of the wife in a pagan marriage becoming a Christian
. . .

"If any of them do not believe the word" describes
those cases where the husbands persistently reject the
call of "the word," a technical designation for the
Christian gospel. Either during public evangelistic
meetings or visits by the missionary to the home, both
husband and wife had been confronted with the call
of the gospel of Christ. The wife experienced its saving power by faith, but the husband continued to re-

ject the message. The negative verb, "do not believe" is literally "to be unpersuaded," portrays those who deliberately and persistently set themselves against the claims of the gospel. According to I Peter 2:8, to persist in such a refusal is fatal. Because early Christians believed that the supreme act of disobedience was to refuse to submit to the truth of the gospel, some interpreters propose that the term simply denotes an unbeliever. However, it is more forceful to accept the verb's full meaning. Such an antagonistic attitude toward the gospel created great difficulty for Christian wives, but Peter assured them that the situation was not hopeless.[29]

Professor Hiebert also explains what it means to "win him without a word."

"Without talk," does not mean that the husband's conversion will be affected apart from the Word of the gospel: it alone is God's regenerating agent. Used without the definite article, the noun (*logou*) indicates the oral pleas of the wife. If the husband will not yield to the authoritative spoken word of the gospel, he may be reached by the wife's silent demonstrations of its transforming power in her daily conduct. Instead of trying to coax and argue her husband into becoming a Christian, she will be more effective by quietly living out its saving power before him. His conscience will be forced to admit the presence of a divine power in her faith that he has often mocked.[30]

One of the points that Professor Hiebert made is that Peter is writing to all women to be submissive to their husbands. In the event they are married to an unbeliever, they are to evangelize them by their behavior, not their word. The passage is about evangelism, not about reproof.

If a woman's husband is a Christian, she is his sister in the Lord. Therefore, she is instructed in other passages to help her husband become as much like the Lord Jesus Christ as possible.

> *Better is an open rebuke than love that is concealed.*
> *Proverbs 27:5*

> *Love rejoices in the truth, it does not rejoice in unrighteousness.*
> *I Corinthians 13:6*

> *If your brother sins (Jesus said) go to him privately (gently, respectfully in love with a motive to restore him) and if he repents you have won your brother.*
> *Matthew 18:15, adaptation added*

If a woman is married to an unbeliever, she may appeal to her husband's conscience or reprove her husband based on what is right. Just because a husband is a non-Christian does not mean his wife should not help him to do what is right as much as he will permit. She simply should not usually use Scripture to convict him as he has no capacity to understand spiritual matters (See I Corinthians 2:14). She should not expect her unbelieving husband to act like a believer.

Some women believe themselves to be more holy the more they suffer. This is simply not true. It is foolish to suffer unnecessarily. It is foolish and also unloving not to try to help her Christian husband grow in the Lord. Similarly, it is foolish and also unloving not to try to help her non-Christian husband mature and be the best husband he can be apart from the Lord. It is important that the Titus 2 Woman understand these concepts and clearly explain them to the younger women.

Chapter Summary

This chapter has explained some of the basic biblical concepts regarding biblical submission of a wife to her husband. She is to obey her husband in all things until he asks her to sin. This is not merely outward obedience but gracious (for the Lord) obedience. This is also not "mutual submission only" or "win him without a word" submission.

Because of the quantity of misinformation dispensed regarding submission in the world and in the church, it is especially important that the Titus 2 Woman understand and live out this particular biblical mandate well. It should be her joy and not a burden. It is God's heart for her and for the younger women.

Chapter Nine

Study Questions

1. From memory list the four places in the New Testament where wives are told to be submissive to their husbands. If you cannot remember, look the answer up.

   A.

   B.

   C.

   D.

2. Based on the Scriptures in question number one, list the four reasons <u>why</u> a wife should be biblically submissive to her husband.

   A.

   B.

C.

D.

3. Write one paragraph of explanation (using appropriate Scripture references) for each of the following:

A. The meaning of the Greek word *hupotasso*.

B. God's authority structure in the home.

C. Submission does not mean the wife is inferior to her husband.

D. How to make a godly appeal.

4. What's wrong with the following statements? Use Scripture to back up your answer.

A. According to I Peter 3:5-6, if a husband asks his wife to sin she is to obey and God will hold her husband accountable for the sin.

B. Wives are not required to be submissive in the way they were in Paul's day. Instead, all Christians are to be mutually submissive.

C. Wives are not permitted to say anything to their husbands (Christian or non-Christian) regardless of what the husband says or does.

5. Summarize the three points explained under the heading "Give Biblical Counsel if the Younger Woman's Husband is Sinning."

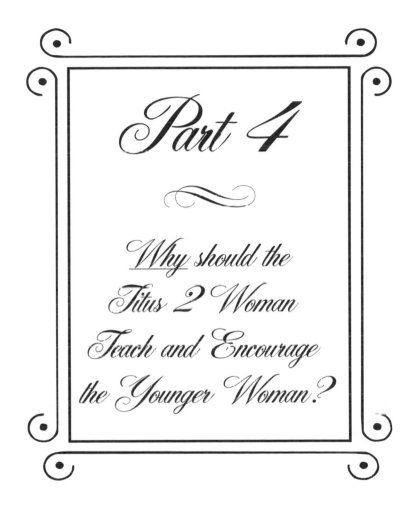

Part 4

Why should the Titus 2 Woman Teach and Encourage the Younger Woman?

Chapter Ten

That the Word of God May Not Be Dishonored

This morning I am babysitting my twin three year old grand-daughters – Kelsey and Jordan. The three of us are sitting with my Mother who is recovering from a broken leg. The girls are bringing so much joy and love into our day. They are full of life and full of curiosity. I do not know how many times in the past two hours either Mother or I have answered the question "What's that?" or "Why?"

Little girls are not the only ones who want to know "Why?". When Paul wrote to Titus with seven specific instructions for the older women to teach the younger women, he also explained why. The reason was simple –

> *. . . that the Word of God may not be dishonored.*
> **Titus 2:5**

The Greek word for dishonored is *blasphemetai*. It means to "speak of with irreverence, to revile or abuse."[31] *Blasphemetai* is a very strong word from which we derive our English word blaspheme. It is not merely remaining neutral towards God's Word. It is an affront to God's Word when women violate any of the seven instructions Paul gave to Titus for the younger women.

The older, Titus 2 Woman should influence the younger woman to bear fruit for the Lord and thus honor His Word. When a young woman's life (or a young man's life or a bondslave's life) has been transformed by God, it is like an advertisement for the gospel.

> *Older women . . . (are to teach) what is good, that they may encourage the young women to love their husbands, to love their children, to be sensible, pure, workers at home, kind, being subject to their own husbands, that the word of God may not be dishonored.*
>
> *Likewise urge the young men to be sensible; in all things show yourself to be an example of good deeds, with purity in doctrine, dignified, sound in speech which is beyond reproach, in order that the opponent may be put to shame, having nothing bad to say about us.*
>
> *Urge bondslaves to be subject to their own masters in everything, to be well-pleasing, not argumentative, not pilfering, but showing all good faith that they may adorn the doctrine of God our Savior in every respect. For the grace of God has appeared, bringing salvation to all men...*
> *Titus 2:5,8,10, emphasis added*

I remember as an unbeliever watching my Christian friends with their families and being envious of them. I was envious because they seemed to have a solid direction and purpose in their lives. They were happy in their circumstances. They seemed to have roots that I did not have. Their lives drew me to the gospel. It was a better advertisement than any billboard could possibly have been.

Just as a godly woman is an advertisement for the gospel, she is bringing honor and not dishonor to God's Word. There are several specific ways mentioned in Titus 2 in which she honors God's Word – when she loves her husband, loves her children, is sensible, pure, a worker at home, kind, and biblically submissive to her husband.

It is also important to remember that a woman honors God's Word when she is submissive, loves her children, is kind, pure, etc. whether she <u>feels</u> like it or not. Consider the example of the Lord Jesus Christ.

> *Therefore, since we have so great a cloud of witnesses surrounding us, let us also lay aside every encumbrance, and the sin which so easily entangles us, and let us run with endurance the race that is set before us, fixing our eyes on Jesus, the author and perfecter of faith, who for the joy set before Him <u>endured the cross, despising the shame,</u> and has sat down at the right hand of the throne of God.*
> *Hebrews 12:1-2, emphasis added*

Like the Lord Jesus, her momentary feelings are inconsequential compared to the joy of being in God's will. The standard which decides her actions is not her feelings, it is God's Word. He, then, receives the honor and the glory. She, therefore, will be given the grace by God to obey Him and her feelings will fade in contrast to His power within her.

Summary

God has given us His Word to embrace. We are to love it and live it before Him. We are to be kind and pure and sensible and all else that God would have us be. The older women are to teach this to the younger women. It is God's high and holy standard for all women. It is the Titus 2 mandate to women. Just the fact that we have the Scriptures is amazing. God has revealed Himself to us through His Word. We should be overwhelmingly grateful to Him for His inspired Word to us. To think and act in any other way is shameful, a dishonor to God, and a dishonor to His Word.

Conclusion

Shortly before Christmas in 1995, we kept our grandchildren so that our daughter Anna and her husband Tom could have a weekend away. Kelsey and Jordan were just over two years old. The day after Anna and Tom left, I noticed that Kelsey was becoming ill. Being a nurse, I examined her only to discover she had swollen glands in her neck. I telephoned Tom (who is a doctor) and asked him to call in a prescription of antibiotics for her. He agreed and I decided to wait until my husband, Sanford, came home from work in about an hour. Then I would go to the drug store and get the medicine. The children were taking a nap.

They were still asleep when Sanford arrived home and I quickly filled him in on what was happening. I got my pocket book and started out the door. Before I got to the car, I decided to go back and check on Kelsey one more time. When I looked into the crib, she was face down so I picked her up. She was limp and had a vacant stare. She was not breathing and her pulse was weak and slow.

I ran with her into our bedroom and told Sanford, "She is not breathing!" He called 911 while I began mouth-to-mouth resuscitation. It was an extremely desperate moment. Several breaths later, she began to breathe on her own. We discovered later that she had very enlarged tonsils and adenoids. As she became acutely ill with the flu, they swelled more thus completely blocking her air passage. God in His mercy and grace spared her life as He used me to literally breathe life back into her. Today she is fine.

As precious as Kelsey's physical life is to me, her spiritual life is even more precious. I know that if I live long enough, God wants to use me to help breathe spiritual life into her, too. Ladies, knowing CPR has value for the here and now but knowing God's Word has value for eternity. Just as it would never occur to you to pass by someone in need of immediate medical help, it should never occur to us to pass by someone in need of spiritual help. The younger women are begging for this help. God requires it. Every woman without Christ is in an extreme, desperate state. Every woman who is not obedient to God's Word is shamefully dishonoring Him. We are responsible before God to help them.

If you have not already, won't you cry out to God and ask Him to make you into a woman who is . . .

> . . . *reverent in (her) behavior, not (a) malicious gossip, nor enslaved to much wine, teaching what is good, that (you) may encourage the young women . . .*
> *Titus 2:3-4, adaptation added*

Chapter Ten

Study Questions

1. What is the meaning of the Greek word *blasphemetai*?

2. Explain biblically the following statement:

    "When a young woman's life has been transformed by God, it is like an advertisement for the gospel."

3. <u>How</u> does a young Christian woman honor the Word of God?
   See Titus 2:3-5

4. Turn back and read your answer to question number one on
   page 4. How, if at all, would your answer differ now?

5. Turn back and read your answer to question number two on page 4. How, if at all, should your priorities differ now?

6. Think back over what you have learned in this study. Do you want to become a Titus 2 Woman? What is your prayer?

Endnotes

[1] James Strong, <u>Strong's Exhaustive Concordance of the Bible</u> (McLean, Virginia: Macdonald Publishing Co.), #2412, p.37.

[2] Matthew Henry, <u>Matthew Henry's Commentary</u> (Grand Rapids, Michigan: Zondervan Publishing House), P.1902.

[3] James Strong, # 1228, p.22.

[4] Robert Thomas, ed., <u>New American Standard Exhaustive Concordance of the Bible</u> (Nashville: Holman Bible Publishers, 1981), # 1402, p. 1644.

[5] Robert Thomas, # 2567, p. 1658.

[6] Ibid.

[7] Robert Thomas, # 4994, p. 1686.

[8] Robert Thomas, # 4998, p. 1686.

[9] Martha Peace, <u>The Excellent Wife</u> (Bemidji, MN: Focus Publishing, 1995), p. 40-42. To obtain a copy of <u>The Excellent Wife</u> book or study guide telephone or FAX Bible Data Services at (770) 486-0011.

[10] Robert Thomas, # 4247, p. 1677.

[11] Robert Thomas, # 5362, p. 1691.

[12] Ibid.

[13] Robert Thomas, # 1515, p. 1645.

[14] Roy Lessin, <u>Spanking: Why, When, How?</u> (Mpls., MN: Bethany House, 1979).

[15] Robert Thomas, #4998, p.1686

[16] The address for Christian Financial Concepts, Inc. is -- P.O. Box 2377, Gainesville, Georgia 30503-2377.

[17] Robert Thomas, #53, p.1627

[18] Robert Thomas, #40, p.1627

[19] Jay Adams, The Handbook of Church Discipline (Grand Rapids, Michigan: Zondervans, 1986).

[20] Robert Thomas, #3626, p.1669.

[21] Martha Peace, p.73-74.

[22] Martha Peace, p.155-174.

[23] John MacArthur, Different by Design (Victor Books, 1994), p.70-71.

[24] Robert Thomas, #18, p.1627.

[25] Robert Thomas, #5293, p.1690.

[26] Martha Peace, p.155-173.

[27] John Piper and Wayne Grudem, Editors, Recovering Biblical Manhood and Womanhood, (Wheaton, Illinois: Crossway Books, 1991), endnotes to chapter eight, number six, p. 493-494.

[28] John MacArthur, New Testament Commentary Ephesians (Chicago: Moody Press,1986), p.282.

[29] D. Edmond Hiebert, 1 Peter (Chicago: Moody Press, 1992), p.196.

[30] D. Edmond Hiebert, p.197

[31] Robert Thomas, #987, p.1638.

Biographical Sketch of Martha Peace

Martha was born, raised, and educated in and around the Atlanta area. She graduated with honors from both the Grady Memorial Hospital School of Nursing 3 year diploma program and the Georgia State University 4 year degree program. She has thirteen years work experience as a Registered Nurse, specializing in pediatric burns, intensive care, and coronary care. She became a Christian in June, 1979. Two years later, Martha ended her nursing career and began focusing her attention on her family and a ladies' Bible study class. For five years she taught verse-by-verse book studies. Then she received training and certification from the National Association of Nouthetic Counselors. N.A.N.C. was started by Dr. Jay Adams for the purpose of training and certifying men and women as biblical counselors.

Martha is a gifted teacher and exhorter. She worked for eight years as a nouthetic counselor at the Atlanta Biblical Counseling Center on Old National Highway, College Park, Georgia, where she counseled women, children, and teenagers. She instructed for 6 years at Carver Bible Institute and College in Atlanta where she taught women's classes including "The Excellent Wife," "Raising Kids Without Raising Cain," "Introduction to Biblical Counseling," "Advanced Biblical Counseling," "Personal Purity," and "The Book of Esther." Martha's books and tapes are available through Bible Data Services, 100 Colt Way, Peachtree City, GA 30269, (770) 486-0011.

Martha is active with her family in Friendship Bible Church in Peachtree City, Georgia, where she teaches teenagers and ladies' Bible study classes. In addition, she conducts seminars for ladies' groups on topics such as "Raising Kids Without Raising Cain," "The Excellent Wife," "Developing a Titus 2 Women's Ministry," "Having a High View of God," and "Personal Purity."

Martha has been married to her high school sweetheart, Sanford Peace, for thirty years. He is an air traffic controller with the FAA but his real work is as an elder at Friendship Bible Church. They have two children: Anna who is married to Tom Scott and lives in Fayetteville, Georgia and David who is married to Jaimee and lives in Peachtree City, Georgia. In addition to their children, they have five grandchildren, Nathan, Caleb, Tommy, and twin baby girls - Kelsey and Jordan.

Study Notes